GOD IS NEAR

8/15/04

To Jake,

Enjoy this book.
Another step on our
journey of faith.

God Bless,
Mary

GOD IS NEAR

Understanding
a Changing Church

Michael Morwood

A Crossroad Book
The Crossroad Publishing Company
New York

The Crossroad Publishing Company
481 Eighth Avenue, New York, NY 10001

First published 1992 by Spectrum Publications Pty Ltd,
Richmond Victoria, Australia

Printed in the United States of America

Library of Congress Cataloging-in-Publication Data
Morwood, Michael.
   God is near : understanding a changing church / Michael
Morwood.
     p. cm.
   Includes bibliographical references.
   ISBN 0-8245-1984-1 (alk. paper)
   1. Spiritual life – Catholic Church. 2. Church. 3. Catholic
Church – Doctrines.   I. Title.
BX2350.3 .M67 2002
248.4′82 – dc21
                                 2002004256

1 2 3 4 5 6 7 8 9 10   08 07 06 05 04 03 02

Contents

Preface

This book is written for people who do not usually read religious books. This creates its own problems, such as how to get such people to read it! I offer it in the hope that it will become known as a book that is informative, easy to read, faithful to the message of Jesus, and, therefore, encouraging. The book will stand or fall on this.

The simplicity of presentation may well be a point of praise if it achieves these aims. It may also be a point of criticism. Criticism will come from those who want every aspect of any issue covered in detail and who will focus on what is left out. I ask the reader to keep in mind that this is not an academic work. The Vatican II document on the Church in the Modern World states that the "split between the faith which many profess and their daily lives deserves to be counted among the more serious errors of our age" (no. 43). I believe that this gap will not be bridged by the use of technical theological language. There is clearly a need for books that use simple language and simple terms to help bridge that gap.

This book invites readers to reflect on their experience of being Christian. At times it will offer something of the church's tradition or teaching, or the insight of a theologian, but these will be offered in a way that invites readers to reflect on their lived experience, in an attempt to bridge the gap Vatican II mentioned. I make no claim to cover or exhaust any topic completely. Rather, I try to offer thoughts that may help readers in their reflection and thinking. I see these pages as opening a door or as indicating a direction rather than providing a detailed coverage of Christian belief.

The central theme of the book is the nearness of our God to us. In order to appreciate this central message of Jesus many of us first will need to ask some questions about the way our faith was shaped:

- How is it (or was it) that Jesus preached that God is near, and yet many of us grew up Christian believing God is *not* near to us?

- How is it that Jesus preached a loving, merciful God, and yet we grew up with a strict Judge-God, a God to be feared?

- How is it that Jesus preached an authority of service, and we grew up with a church authority that seemed aloof, remote, and demanding?

- How is it that the Good News Jesus preached became entangled with law and regulations, and religion became burdensome or irrelevant to many Christians?

- How is it that our Christian faith, which should be a privilege for us and a source of great peace and encouragement, is experienced by many Christians as a burden, as something restrictive, and, as such, is rejected?

This is not to suggest that following Jesus should be without pain, struggle, and burden. It *is* difficult to live and love as Jesus challenges us to. The mistake we have made all too often, though, has been to separate the encouraging teaching of Jesus from whatever struggle we face. It is the mistake of moving our focus from Jesus' central teaching that God is loving and is close to us in all that happens. Whenever the church has done that, the faithful have found themselves experiencing separation from God and relating with God as if they had not yet heard "Good News." Many of our liturgical prayers, for example, still suggest that God is not with us or is yet to reach out to help us.

I believe that reflection on this central truth of our faith — God's nearness to us — is the key factor in understanding a changing church. Reflecting on whatever has been our experience of God's closeness to us and the way that has been shaped will help us as we look at the kind of church that we are called to create together as God's people. If we can understand our past, the way it was shaped and factors influencing changes in the present, we will be on a solid foundation to shape the future. More and more Christians in every local community will need to be involved in this process if we are to shape a worthwhile church for the future. Many of these Christians do not read religious books, but I hope they might be led to read this one, and that their reading, reflection, and further discussion might help in some way in shaping that worthwhile church community we all desire.

While writing this book I often had in mind my sisters and my brothers who have nurtured and supported me in life's journey. I thank them for the gifts of simplicity and common sense.

To the Missionaries of the Sacred Heart I express thanks likewise for nurture and support, and for the gift of discovering the love of God revealed in the humanness of Jesus.

To Madeleine Barlow, Frank Andersen, Maria Kelly, Pat Synnott, and Maria Rohr I express not only my thanks but also my admiration for their patience in working on the manuscript with me. I know this book would never have reached publication without their help.

In general, Scripture quotes are taken from the Jerusalem Bible.

New Edition 2002

The revisions in this edition focus mainly on language rather than ideas, and the changes are found mainly in the first two chapters. In the first chapter I have retained traditional or popular language concerning "heaven" and "getting to heaven" in order to link with how many Christians would speak about this topic. Throughout the text I have changed from speaking of Jesus "with" or "in" us to "the same Spirit that moved in Jesus moving in us." In reediting I have also kept in mind a general "Christian" readership rather than the "Catholic" audience the original edition addressed.

The greatest shift in my own thinking in the past ten years has to do with whether we understand Jesus as someone who rescued a fallen race exiled from God, or as someone who opened our minds and eyes to the fact of God's gracious presence with all people in all places at all times. This book does not develop this shift in my thinking, but I have changed words or phrases in the original text that suggest the former understanding. An expanded treatment of this development can be found in *Tomorrow's Catholic: Understanding God and Jesus in a New Millennium* (Mystic, Conn.: Twenty-Third Publications, 1997) and *Is Jesus God? Finding Our Faith* (New York: Crossroad, 2001).

Chapter One

The God Who Is Near to Us

The two reflective exercises on this page are simple
and brief. Please take a few moments to do them
before reading this chapter.

1. Consider how close you are to God. Give yourself
   a mark on a scale of one to ten indicating how close
   you think you are.

2. Give yourself a mark from one to ten indicating
   how sure you are of getting to "heaven," eternal
   life with God.

O UR RESPONSES to these two exercises can reveal
to us something about our image of God and our
relationship with God.

I have often used these two exercises with groups of
adult Catholics. Very few have had an average mark for
either exercise above six. This seems to indicate that it is
fairly general for Catholics to believe that they are not close
to God. It also seems to indicate a doubt about reaching
heaven, understood as a state of eternal life with God.

Our responses can point to a difficulty we have in recog-
nizing that God is close to us and that eternal life is God's
gift to us. If, for example, we were to turn the first exercise around and ask God, "How close are you to each one
of us?" the response would obviously be ten out of ten.
Our God could not be any closer. Our difficulty is in being
aware of this closeness.

God *is* ten-out-of-ten close to us. That *is* the reality of
our lives. Heaven is God's gift to us; we do not acquire
eternal life with God by our effort. These are fundamental truths of our religion. Why do we have difficulty
believing them?

The difficulty may lie in the fact that all too many of us
have inherited a viewpoint that looks on God as a *goal* to be
reached. We have become deeply entrenched in this understanding. This leads us to focus our efforts on bridging the
gap between God and ourselves. Basically, it implies that

when we get our act together and become better than we
are now, we will then be close to God.

Consider whether any of the following ideas or attitudes
ring true to your experience of being raised Christian:

- Life is seen as a journey *to* God.

- There has been heavy emphasis on my need to stop
  sinning if I am to bridge the gap between the sacred
  and myself.

- I must do good, pray more, acquire virtue, get rid of
  my faults, and *then* I will be close to God.

- I believe that my performance, my good efforts, *win*
  God's approval and reward.

- I learned to distrust the body, as if the body is sinful. Consequently any enjoyment of my sexuality
  sometimes leaves me feeling guilty.

- I have a sense of the wide gap between the world in
  which I live and what is sacred.

- Prayer is an effort to bridge this gap between myself
  and God "out there."

- Over all this, like a blanket, is the sense of my poor
  effort, my sin, my failure to make progress.

- The emphasis in Scripture seems to be on the importance of taking up my cross and walking the
  narrow path.

- My image of meeting God in death has been associated with the scales of justice. I will know only then
  whether my good deeds will outweigh the bad.

- At times I find myself wondering if I've done enough to "get to heaven."

A simple diagram will illustrate this way of viewing our relationship with God:

Life: A Journey to God

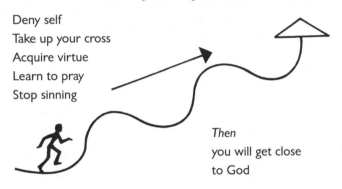

Deny self
Take up your cross
Acquire virtue
Learn to pray
Stop sinning

Then
you will get close
to God

The diagram illustrates a common Christian viewpoint about life and God: here am I on my journey through life, journeying to God. The journey is like a climb up a mountain: the more work I do, the closer I will get to the top. So in the spiritual journey toward God it appears that the more I do and the better I become, the closer I will get to God. Sometimes I seem to make progress and I experience closeness to God; at other times I feel that I have slipped back. What an uphill battle it is! And how discouraging!

The pity is that so many of us will recognize our own experience in the above summary. It is a pity because, although it is an overview of common Christian experience, it needs to be labeled as thoroughly unchristian. One sad consequence is that many elderly Christians — thoroughly good people — wonder in their old age if they have done enough "to win a place in heaven."

The viewpoint that we must reclaim is that of the Gospels (literally the "Good News"):

- Life is a journey *with* our God.
- I am a "temple of God's Holy Spirit."
- My God not only embraces me, but is with me in the depths of my being.
- God is never absent from me.
- God will never stop loving me.
- I am created in the image of God, who is Love.
- I do not *deserve* God's goodness or eternal life with God. I do not *earn* them. They are God's *gift* to me.

Another simple diagram illustrates this Gospel viewpoint:

Life: A Journey *with* God

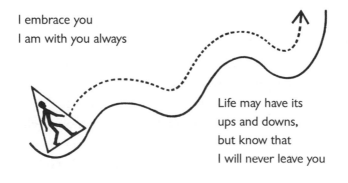

I embrace you
I am with you always

Life may have its ups and downs, but know that I will never leave you

The diagram illustrates what Scripture calls us to believe: I am a dwelling place of the sacred ... *now!*

Paul wrote to the Corinthians:

> Didn't you realize that you were God's temple,
> and that the Spirit of God is living among you?
>
> (1 Cor. 3:16)

The First Letter of John states clearly this foundational truth of Christianity:

> We ourselves have known
> and put our faith in God's love toward ourselves.
> God is love,
> and if you live in love, you live in God
> and God lives in you. (4:16)

The truth is that in this life I will never get closer to God than I am *now.* God loves me totally *now.* God will not love me any more in ten years' time no matter what great things I might do. God's love will not change. What can change is my awareness of God's presence with me and love for me. The difference between myself and the greatest of the saints is not that any one of them was closer to God in life than I am. The difference lies in their sensitive awareness of God's loving presence. It is this awareness and belief that leads the saints to respond in such extraordinary ways. This extraordinary change in ordinary people is the highlight of the church's beginnings. Those early Christians believed the Good News and were ready to take on the world because of that belief. They had an unshakeable conviction that their God was intimately close to them. They knew they were "earthen vessels," to use Paul's phrase, capable of failure and sin, fragile, and easily broken. But they knew, too, that they "held a treasure" (2 Cor. 4:7), the treasure of God's presence.

The heart of the matter for us as Christians is whether we can proclaim that we know and put our faith in God's love for us and God's presence with us. Paul, writing to the Corinthians, gave them a simple test of their faith:

> Examine yourselves to make sure you are in the faith.
> Test yourselves.
> Do you acknowledge that Jesus Christ is really in you?
> If not, you have failed the test. (2 Cor. 13:5)

In the light of these foundational truths, look at the answers you gave at the beginning of this chapter. The scores most people give themselves suggest they believe they are not doing enough to get close to God. The scores suggest an underlying belief that God's love and happiness with God in eternity have to be won by one's own efforts. It is not unusual for people believing this to feel a sense of failure and to carry in themselves a sense of their distance from God, even when they are very good people. What is needed is the realization that they are considering their relationship with God from the wrong viewpoint. Jesus, the bearer of Good News, invites us to believe in a far more encouraging reality. Each one of us, though, has to work at deepening our awareness of and our belief in these foundational truths:

> God loves me — *now;*
> God is intimately present with me — *now.*

In fact, God could not be more present to me than God is now. Nor is God more present to any other person on earth than God is present to me. The key is *awareness of this presence.* When I deepen my awareness and belief, my basic response will be accompanied with gratitude and joy. This awareness will in turn affect the way I respect myself and respect others. There will also be the conviction that nothing and no one can take this gift from me. Life will have its ups and downs, but God's presence is constant whether I feel it or am conscious of it or not.

But ... I can refuse to believe this Good News of God's presence.

Isn't this almost unbelievable?

Isn't it a pity that there are some people in the church who are so hung up on the possibility of turning from God, so focused on sin, that they never, as it were, open themselves in loving and grateful joy to accept the gift of God's transforming presence in them?

The Gift of Heaven

"Heaven" is eternal life with God. Our images suggest it is a place, somewhere above us, but today we find our simple images being challenged by what we know about the universe. Beyond the images, though, is our belief in life beyond here, eternal life with God, and connection between the way life is lived here and life hereafter. How sure are you of getting to heaven, however you imagine heaven to be? Call to mind your response to the second question at the beginning of this chapter. If the answer is not ten, why not?

Some people are ready to jump up and say, "But you cannot presume that!"

In doing so, they miss a central point of Christian faith: we profess to believe in an eternal connectedness between living in love and living in God. We live in love, we live in God; we die in love, we die into God. Dying into God is not something we "win" or something anyone "wins" for us. No, we believe we die into God because this is who and how God is. In other words, we believe our very existence is intertwined with God's graciousness.

It is heresy to believe that I win my way to heaven.

Many Christians, however, live as if they had to win eternal life with God through the good they do, the prayers they say, the novenas they make, the religious services they attend, the penances they endure — even the boring homilies they sit through! Some even believe there will be a strict "judgment" at the time of death to determine whether they will gain access to God's presence. Consequently, the practice of their religion often seems more burdensome than joyful, something privatized rather than something involving others, a struggle to get somewhere rather than a response to God's loving presence with us.

Note two things here. First, it is time we stopped imagining that when we die we are going to go to "another place" ("heaven") where God really lives. No, we exist now *in* God. Death will be a time of transformation — a different way of existing or "living on" *in* God. We Christians have a lot of work to do in reshaping our imagination about what happens at death. We have to shift from images (very prominent throughout Christian history) that suggest that God's "home" is elsewhere, especially "up above" us in a place we've called "heaven."

Second, it is time also for us to stop imagining a time of judgment when God decides who gets "in" and who does not get "in." Look at Jesus' image again. God is not deciding who is a sheep and who is a goat. No, we will die either a "sheep" or a "goat." We should be trusting all through our lives that we have no intention of turning our backs on being decent human beings and that we will — along with anyone else on earth who lives "in love" — die into eternal life with God.

God's Goodness

God is present to us. This presence has an eternal dimension to it. These truths could change our lives. The reality is that we have a God who, in effect, says to each of us:

> Life may be tough for you, but I assure you now that heaven is my gift to you. It is a safe gift. All I ask is that you live life, whatever life holds for you, believing in the gift and in my love for you, and that you try to love others with the same abundant love with which I love you.

The Good News is that we will lose the gift only if we *refuse* it. Such a refusal would have to be one of the most critical decisions we could make. The loss of eternal life with God does not result from isolated sins or the reality of our constant weakness. It is a matter of making ourselves incapable of embracing at the end of our lives the God who is pure Love. It is to choose a path of such malice and evil in life that one *could not* then reach out to accept God's love at death. Death will be the moment in which we walk into — or finally reject — God's loving embrace. The way we now live prepares us for that moment. Here and now each of us is determining, through the way we love, our capacity to be filled with Love itself.

Confidence in God's Goodness

We live basically good and decent lives. Deep in our hearts we *know* we will return the embrace. We are good people in spite of our faults, our sins, and our failures. At the very least we can say· "At this moment of my life I have no intention whatever of turning my back on God's love." We would do well to trust in this basic goodness and in our basic desire to do good. In John's Gospel we read: "No one who believes in Jesus will be condemned" (3:18). Why not? Because no one can genuinely *believe in* Jesus without being open to love and goodness. You cannot "believe in" Jesus and at the same time reject God.

Such trust and a positive attitude to meeting God in death would surely make a difference to the nature and quality of our religious practice. A pagan philosopher once said he couldn't believe in Christianity because Christians did not look or act as if they were redeemed! They were joyless and grim in going about their religious duties. The same sort of grim, joyless Christianity is still to be found today. It still has a strong presence in the church. It is found in the widespread attitude that says religion has to be tough and difficult. Indeed the "tough old days" mentality still holds strong appeal for many. They assert that it is all made too easy nowadays. But is it?

Let us examine again the two different approaches to God and consider the responsibilities that each places upon us.

The "Life as a Journey *to*" model basically says:

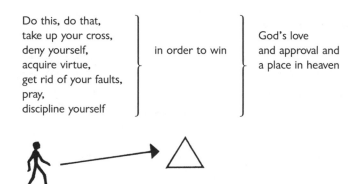

| Do this, do that, take up your cross, deny yourself, acquire virtue, get rid of your faults, pray, discipline yourself | in order to win | God's love and approval and a place in heaven |

There is an emphasis here on keeping the law, on strictness, and on winning one's way to heaven. It highlights the sense of distance between us and God and the struggle to overcome it. It can be filled with discouragement, looks rather grim, and can promote a poor self-image. There can be no denying that this model produced people of extraordinary faith. What is lamentable is the other side of the story: many Christians found this style of religion discouraging, restrictive, and joyless.

The "Life as a Journey *with*" model is based on:

God's love for
and presence
with us.

This is affirmed in baptism and the fact that we are created in the image of our God.

But we still *must:*

Do this and that,
take up our cross,
deny ourselves,
acquire virtue,   in order to
get rid of our faults,
pray,
and discipline ourselves

allow this "life" to grow
to deepen our awareness
   of God with us
respond faithfully
witness by our loving
spread the Good News

The hard work and the struggle are still there. Life does not suddenly become a bed of roses. Life may have enormous struggles for us to deal with. But the difference is the peace of knowing that I do not have to struggle to get to God. It is quite wrong to assert, as some Christians are quick to do, that the changes in our thinking about God have made things too easy, as if Christianity has been watered down to suit anyone's taste.

Need for Balance

The challenge to accept the Good News about our God
is not an invitation to take the easy way out. Christianity
has two very important factors that have to be kept in
balance constantly. First, we have to listen to, accept, and
be convinced of the Good News of God's love for us and
God's presence with us. This is meant to be encouraging
and uplifting. But Christianity cannot stop there. I cannot,
as a Christian, then find a corner to settle in, make life easy
and comfortable, and let the world go by. That is not Christianity! Rather, I deepen my belief, and then I am called to
respond. I am called to love God and my neighbor. I am
called to love as Jesus loved. There is nothing easy about
that! I am called to work, as Jesus did, for a better and more
just society. I am, in effect, asked to be present in the world
as Jesus would be. There are tremendous challenges in that.

We make mistakes if we fail to keep this balance. Christianity too often has laid burdens on people by preaching
the cross and the struggle without proper regard for the
Good News that is meant to uplift and encourage. On the
other hand, there is the danger, especially in our local communities today, that we preach and settle for "comforting
good news" rather than move on to the challenges that face
us if we are to respond as God would want us to.

Mortal Sin

One topic often raised in Catholic circles in the light of
the material in this chapter is mortal sin. This is to be ex-

pected since the topic deals with whether we are close to God or not and whether we will be able to return God's loving embrace in death. Sin often surfaces along with the "watering down" charge some Catholics make about the church today. How are we to understand "mortal" sin?

It was so clear once: we had a list of things that were mortal sins. Mortal sin was automatically linked with certain actions. Many Catholics, accustomed to viewing mortal sin in this light, are now confused when actions they considered to be mortal sin, especially missing Mass on Sunday, are not viewed with the same seriousness by their children or others. They see this as a weakening of discipline. It seems to be the easy way out.

It is not a watering down. The church's understanding of mortal sin since the Council of Trent has been clear and definite: mortal sin is that sin whereby someone with full intent and deliberation, in a serious matter, *decides to cut himself or herself off from God*. Pope John Paul II wrote:

> With the whole tradition of the church, we call mortal sin the act by which man freely and consciously rejects God, his law, the covenant of love that God offers, preferring to turn in on himself or to some created and finite reality, something contrary to the divine will ... in a grave matter. ... Man perceives that this disobedience to God destroys the bond that unites him with his life principle: it is a mortal sin, that is, an act which gravely offends God and ends in turning against man himself with a dark and powerful force of destruction.[1]

To recognize mortal sin, we ask: Was the intention malicious or evil, and was there a deliberate decision to cut oneself off from God? Maybe we would then discover that some of the actions we have considered as "mortal sin" are not so "deadly" after all. Today Catholic moral teaching on mortal sin is not simply taking the easy way out. Rather, it is helping us to see that we cannot simply call certain actions "mortal sin" without reference to a definite decision to cut our ties with God and turning to "a dark and powerful force of destruction" that would make us *incapable* of walking into Love's embrace at death.

Our sense of sin, especially serious sin, has to be linked with our awareness of God's love for us and the way we are choosing to live in relationship with God. Too often we have had mortal sin hung around our necks and have thought ourselves damned to hell when in reality we never had any intention whatever of cutting ourselves off from God.

Serious Sin

Part of our difficulty stems from the clear distinction between mortal and venial sins. It forced us to call anything of a serious nature "mortal sin," even when there was no clear intention of turning our backs on God. It would help our thinking if we reserved "mortal" sin to its strict definition: the sin of *death* because it is an attitude that seeks to cut oneself off completely from God. We could then refer to other sins as "serious" according to their capacity to cause harm to oneself and others.

Better Scoring!

God's nearness to us and God's love for us are Good News. Our task is to get that first score at the beginning of this chapter up to nine or ten so that we can affirm, "Yes. I am very, very close to God." We will be able to affirm that, not because we have done great things, but because God is always with us and we have grown in our awareness of this truth. The final chapter on prayer may help with this growth. Likewise, we should affirm with confidence that we do not intend to refuse God's gift of heaven. Therefore, we can and should live with some confidence that we are going to joyfully return Love's waiting embrace when we die.

The Important Question

This chapter began with a reflection on the two questions:

- How close do you consider you are to God?
- How sure are you of getting to heaven ?

If Christians scored themselves highly on these two questions, what a difference this would make to the way we gather for worship. It would strengthen the bonds that unite us, improve the quality of our prayer, and stimulate our concern to share the Good News with others. On the other hand, if the average score of the majority of Christians remains low, then these questions immediately confront us:

- What sort of God do we believe in?
- What are we witnessing to in our religion?

- Why would we expect anyone to be attracted to our religion?

- Why should we be surprised if many Christians find their religion uninspiring, irrelevant, or just simply dull and lifeless?

It is not enough to take refuge in oughts and shoulds. The important question is this: as individuals or as a community are we witnessing clearly and with vitality to the presence of God with us?

Summary

- Life is a journey *with* God.

- God is never absent from me.

- God loves me totally, freely, *now.*

- Heaven is God's gift to me.

- God asks me to live believing in these gifts.

- The heart of the matter for me as a Christian is whether I can proclaim that I know and put my faith in God's love for me and God's presence with me (see the First Letter of John, chapter 4).

- When I deepen my awareness and belief, my basic response will be accompanied by gratitude and joy.

- Hard work, struggle, and the acceptance of responsibility are part of life. The difference is the peace of knowing that I do not have to struggle to get to God.

- There is nothing easy in being asked to love others the way God loves me!

- Actions cannot be called "mortal sin" without reference to evil intent and a definite decision to cut ties with God.

Chapter Two

Jesus: Revealer of
the Nearness of God

Before reading this chapter, consider the following statements and whether you would respond with "Yes," "No," or "Unsure" to each of them.

1. At the birth of Jesus, Mary knew he was God.

2. At the age of four, Jesus would have known he was God.

3. Jesus was human like us in *everything* except sin.

4. Jesus was tempted to sexual sins.

5. Jesus would have known that the continent we call America existed.

6. Jesus sometimes broke religious laws.

7. Jesus had to live by *faith,* just as we do.

8. The Gospel stories of Jesus' birth are factual, historical accounts of what took place.

9. Jesus liked some people more than others.

10. Jesus experienced doubt, pain, loneliness, and disappointment the way we do.

T WO OF THE GREAT "mysteries" in traditional Christian doctrine are the mystery of the Trinity and the mystery of Jesus who is both divine and human.

The mystery of the Trinity does not seem to trouble most Christians very much. They tend to accept that three in one is somewhat beyond them; they accept the understanding that God is three, yet one. They don't understand this fully, but their lack of understanding does not seem to create problems for them. They are fairly content to accept the mystery and the wonder of it, knowing they are not going to solve the contradiction that seems to be there.

The second great mystery — Jesus, human and divine — is far more problematical.

The problems arise when we try to solve the mystery that Jesus is really human, human like us in all things (except sin), and that Jesus is divine. Our efforts to bring the divine and the human together in Jesus are often done in such a way that we have a Divine Superman, a God-man walking the earth in Jesus' sandals. We must not, though, allow the divine reality, however we understand it, to swamp the human reality so that Jesus is no longer human, and limited, like us.

St. Augustine has given us very simple but very good advice. He wrote of Jesus, "Walk in the man, and you will arrive at God." St. Thomas Aquinas wrote, "In his humanity he is the way.... If you seek to know what path to follow, take Christ because he is the way: 'This is the way, walk in it.' "[2] In this chapter we will try to "walk in the man" Jesus. We will then arrive at Jesus, raised to fullness of life with God.

The Birth of Jesus

Our starting point is the birth of Jesus. We immediately encounter a problem here with the scriptural accounts of his birth. The presence of angels, shepherds, and Magi suggests to our minds that God is being revealed to the world at the time of the birth.

We need to be aware that the stories of Jesus' birth are colored by the knowledge the writers acquired after his Resurrection. The accounts of the birth are written through "Savior-tinted" glasses, as it were. The important point for the Gospel writers was not the actual details of the birth, but the truth that Jesus is Lord and Savior, a truth not revealed fully until the Resurrection. The respected *Jerome Biblical Commentary* in the article on Luke's Gospel provides an understanding of how the infancy stories, not in the first Gospel, Mark, came to be written:

> [Matthew, Luke, and John] add some kind of "infancy gospel" to their major undertaking. . . . That these "infancy narratives" were not an original part of the apostolic preaching can be established, not only from the fact that Jesus' redemptive ministry began only with the baptism by John but also from the fact that the apostles' ministry depended on what they

had seen as eyewitnesses. In preaching, the apostles *worked backward* from Pentecost to the resurrection to the passion and death to the public ministry and eventually to the "hidden life" of Jesus. The infancy narratives emerged out of the endeavor to import an even fuller understanding of the redemptive work and words of Jesus. (no. 21; emphasis added)

Many of us were raised without this understanding of how the Gospels were composed. Without an understanding of the way the infancy narratives were added to the early preaching and the Gospels we can fall into the mistake of seeing Jesus revealed as God even at birth.

Our Christmas cribs, for example, often convey the message that Mary and Joseph knew the divinity of Jesus as this came to be understood later. Many cribs have Mary and Joseph in a position of prayer adoring their God. It is not surprising, then, that we grew up with the belief that Mary knew her child was God. The Gospels, too, seem to be clear that Mary knew! But then we come back to the point that whatever the Gospels share about the divinity of Jesus was insight gained after the Resurrection and written back into the stories of his life.

It will come as quite a surprise to many Catholics, then, that the *Jerome Biblical Commentary* suggests that Mary would not have known her child was divine in the way Christians came to think of his divinity. Paragraph 32 in the section on Luke's Gospel gives several reasons for this:

- Luke's treatment of the Annunciation is not giving a diary of the day, but a Gospel of salvation.

- As a Jew Mary would not be thinking in our terms of a Trinity.

- There are indications that before Pentecost Mary did not fully appreciate the mission of Jesus.

- The Old Testament does not write of the expected Messiah as divine.

This information may come as a surprise to us because we are accustomed to thinking of the birth of Jesus in a different light. Often people react strongly when long-held beliefs, especially religious ones, are questioned, or when invited to look at an issue in a different light. Such change can be confusing. On the other hand, this information is a good example of how scholarship challenges us to a different understanding. The truth is that Jesus' divinity as understood by the Christian tradition was not clearly articulated until well after he died. We should not read the infancy accounts as if the birth were revealing or proving this much later understanding.

Mary

An appreciation that Christian understanding of Jesus' divinity was not articulated until after the Resurrection gives us a different perspective on Mary. If she knew her child was God, then, really, life must have been a breeze! Imagine what it must be like to have God at your feet, God growing up in your home! And of course, there would be nothing to be afraid of with God around. Even the fact of her son taking on the religious leaders of the nation would be nothing to worry about. The crucifixion of Jesus becomes simply a time of waiting. It would not bewilder nor break the mother's heart: the God-Jesus is really safe.

What if it was *not* like that? What if Mary was like any other mother raising her son, filled with plans and dreams, wondering what the future might hold? Granted that Mary came to believe that her son was special in God's eyes and had a special task to perform, what would it have been like for her when all her relatives and friends rejected him, when he was seen as a troublemaker by the religious leaders?

Mary was a woman raised in the Old Testament. What must it have been like for her to have her son question publicly many practices that must have been dear to her? Did she ever wonder if he was going too far, or that he might be mistaken? Had she believed that Jesus was God incarnate, there would have been no problem. But having to have faith in her son in the midst of searching, uncertainty, and rejection makes Mary's experience of faith far closer to our own experience as people of faith.

Like any human mother Mary would have looked to the future with questions and dreams, "pondering in her heart." She spent many years with her son, watching him grow and develop. She had to let him go, and then watch as he was rejected by his relations and all at Nazareth who wanted to "put him away because they thought he was out of his mind" (Mark 3:21). She would have watched, surely with some anxiety, as he clashed with the religious leaders, as people rejected him, as he faced defeat and failure. She was present at the foot of the cross, one imagines with almost unbearable pain in her heart, and had to hope and believe that sometime, somehow, God's activity would make sense of the failure, the brutality, the hardness of heart, the loneliness, the lack of understanding, and the rejection.

Not knowing with certainty but believing in faith makes Mary's position at the foot of the cross very different: How close she was then to us and to our struggle to believe in God's goodness in the face of tragedy and human cruelty.

Jesus, Human Like Us

Now think of Jesus. If Jesus knows everything God knows, then he does not have to live by faith; there is no un-certainty, no questioning, no searching, no act of faith required in times of doubt and darkness. However, for Jesus to be really human, he must live by faith. That is an essential part of being human.

It is not uncommon at this point for some people to interject and say, "But he is *God!*" and their thinking makes it very difficult for them to stay with the reality of Jesus be-ing human. They hear a denial of divinity where no denial is intended. The issue is that we cannot defend the divinity of Jesus at the expense of denying his humanness. St. Au-gustine's advice, mentioned earlier, would urge patience, along with an open, inquiring mind concerning the reality of Jesus being human. It is from this human experience that we are to learn about God.

A difficulty in accepting the human Jesus comes from the fact that in traditional and popular thinking Christians have used the Gospel stories to *prove* that Jesus is God. We were led to the miracles and to many passages in John's Gospel in particular, and it all seemed so clear: Jesus must have known he was God.

It would help if we kept several points in mind.

First, the miracles do not prove that Jesus is God. Look at the speech of Peter in chapter 2 of the Acts of the Apostles: "Jesus the Nazarene was a man commended to you by God by the miracles and portents and signs *that God worked through him*" (v. 22). The miracles were used by the early followers of Jesus to demonstrate God worked in and through him, not to prove that he was God.

Second, John's Gospel is very much a Gospel about Jesus who is *Risen Lord and Light of the World* rather than being a biography of Jesus the *man*. John's Gospel is a theology of Jesus, a theology shaped in the light of the Resurrection and the worldview of the time. Its concern is to demonstrate *who we now believe Jesus to be* rather than *what actually happened*. The "I am" statements, the long discourses, and the chapters on the Last Supper all demonstrate this concern. This should not disturb us if we appreciate that the Gospels were faith documents, not biographies of Jesus. They were written to cement faith in particular communities. The literary device of putting words and even speeches back onto Jesus' lips was simply a way of expressing their faith in and theology about Jesus. John's Gospel invites us today to share that same faith and theology.

Third, rather than go to the Gospels to prove that Jesus is God, we should be more concerned with going to the Gospels to learn what we can about God from the life and teaching of this extraordinary man.

Let Jesus Be Human

If we want to meet the human Jesus, we must let him be human! We need to stop the tape that continually plays within our minds, telling us over and over, "But he was God . . . it was different . . . he was God." We need to appreciate as fully as we can the reality of his humanity.

Let us return to the birth of Jesus. This baby is helpless, dependent, unaware of the world around him. Like any other human child he will grow in awareness and learn to walk, to speak, and to relate.

If we want to meet the human Jesus, we could begin by asking him some basic questions, questions we have probably never thought to ask him. How did you cut your fingernails? Did you get blisters on your feet? Did the mule you rode ever get lame? Did you get dust in your eyes and your eyes get sore and bloodshot? Did you ever get so tired that all you wanted to do was stop and sleep? Did you wonder as you grew up what you wanted to be when you were a man? Did you ever long to be held by a woman? Did you want to marry?

Such questions are not trivial. They can help break down our image of the "superhuman" Jesus who breezes through life, untouched by the realities and the questions that are so much part of our human existence.

What was the day-to-day effect of Joseph and Mary on Jesus? Through Joseph did he not experience that a father's love and care are a child's best model for belief in a God he called "Father"?

From both Mary and Joseph did he not acquire a

sense of God's presence? Wouldn't *their faith* have given him an insight into who God is and the conviction that God's kingdom is characterized by unbelievable mercy and compassion? Surely it was from the love between Joseph and Mary that he learned his own deep and radical understanding of love.

We can and should use the human experiences common to Jesus and ourselves as stepping stones between our hearts and his heart. This is how we can know him better, how our hearts and his heart can touch, and how we can develop genuine friendship with him. Otherwise we run the risk of having a Jesus whose heart we cannot know, someone who is not really like us.

"Completely Like Us"?

Jesus grew up in Nazareth, a tough place — nothing good came from there the Gospels tell us. We would do well to reflect on these years, letting our own experience of growing up guide us and help us span both the culture and the time gap. Did he know exactly what God wanted of him? Well, do we know exactly what God wants of us? Is not that uncertainty part of being human? Why, then, do we so often think of Jesus as walking in certainty? Do we really believe the words of Scripture:

> It was essential that he should in this way become completely like his brothers, so that he could be a compassionate and trustworthy high priest.
>
> (Heb. 2:17–18)

> For it is not as if we have a high priest who was
> incapable of feeling our weaknesses with us; but we
> have one who has been tempted in every way that we
> are, though he is without sin. (Heb. 4:15)

What an extraordinary text! Do we really believe that Jesus
has been tempted in every way that we are? Do we see
Jesus' temptations as a once only event on a grand scale
during forty days in the desert or do we see him being
tempted all through life up till his death on the cross? Have
we ever tried to converse with Jesus about the subtlety and
the attractiveness of temptation and the inner struggle to
resist it?

Jesus the Teacher

People who listened to Jesus perceived that he spoke with
an authority different from that of other religious leaders.
He spoke with an authority that grew out of his experience
of being human, of knowing temptation, of living without power, without influence, without status, without the
means to achieve all he dreamed of achieving. He knew
what it was like to rub shoulders with and to share the
lot of the truly "poor" who were put down by those who
had power. He knew what it was like to live by faith. He
did not speak as someone speaking down to people, but as
someone with conviction born of experience, prayer, and
faith. So his "Beatitudes" are the conviction of a man who
knew what it was like to be poor in spirit, who mourned,
who was pure of heart, who sought peace, who had all

sorts of calumny spoken against him. He knew what it was like to be hungry and to be fed, to be lonely and be to comforted or given shelter. These experiences of his own living form the foundation of the ultimate blessing as Jesus perceived it: "Come, you have my Father's blessing . . . for when I was hungry or thirsty, or a stranger, naked, ill, or in prison . . . when you did [this] for one another, you did it to me" (Matt. 25).

His parables have the persuasion of a man who has sought the hidden treasure, or the pearl of great price, and devoted his life to this treasure, whatever the cost. In his own living and preaching Jesus shows that it is the person who can say, "I've been there," who can speak with conviction and authority about faith and hope.

The Message of Jesus

Jesus surprised and shocked the religious leaders of his day by his clear and direct teaching that God is near to the poor and the outcasts. Even sinners, he taught, would find a warm and loving response in God if they turned to God sincerely.

In simple language and with simple ideas Jesus spoke to the crowds of a God who is merciful, loving, ready to forgive, and caring. Jesus invited people to trust in this God, the way a child would trust a most loving parent. He told parables that would have seemed crazy to his listeners:

A shepherd leaving ninety-nine sheep and going after one stray? And then to carry the stray sheep home!

> No beating, no dragging by the scruff of the neck,
> no kick in the tail?

> A father who would divide his property and allow the
> younger son to depart and squander the inheritance?
> Then to embrace him on his return!

These are not just simple, lovely stories. With these stories
Jesus intended to jolt his listeners into a different way of
thinking about their God. The punishment, the scolding,
the setting apart we expect do not feature. It seems too
good to be true.

Another feature of Jesus' description of God is the way
he linked it to the listeners' experience of being parents. He
invited them to see that if they could be loving, forgiving,
and generous with their children how much more could they
trust God to be loving and forgiving toward themselves.

Conversion

Jesus calls us to a conversion. Fundamentally, this is a
turning around of the ways we think about and image
God, leading to sharper belief in and awareness of God's
presence with and love for us. Conversion will then make
itself evident in the way we relate with God and with one
another.

It is significant, in this regard, that the first words Jesus
speaks in Mark's Gospel, the first of the Gospels, are:

> The time has come and the kingdom of God is close
> at hand. Repent, and believe the Good News. (1:15)

Why repent? Why be converted? So that we might believe the Good News! Isn't it striking how positive that is!

Indeed, Jesus' ministry is characterized by this positive stance. He asks people to think positively about God and about themselves. Peter is a good example of this. Peter, who thought he was too much of a sinner to have anything to do with Jesus; Peter, who failed so miserably; Peter, who eventually came to believe that Jesus could see beyond his failure and recklessness and have trust in him.

The pattern of Jesus' preaching is relevant to our church today: preach the Good News — preach it wholeheartedly — and then challenge the hearers to respond. Maybe people are failing to respond today to the degree that the church is not seen to be preaching Good News.

Losing Sight of Jesus

It is a sad and tragic feature of Catholic history that the religion meant to keep this Good News alive in the world and to encourage believers' response to it lost sight of this focus in its teaching and in its practice. The history of the Eucharist clearly shows this, as we shall see in the next chapter. The images we have associated with death and judgment, for example, have been shaped more by the fanciful imagination and the fearful mentality of the Middle Ages than by the teaching of Jesus. Contrast the embrace of the Prodigal Son and the father's joy at his return with the fear that has surrounded our approach to death. The Catholic Church for centuries was seen to put its focus on limbo, purgatory, hell, indulgences, and a fearful God, rather than on the God Jesus describes. Catholic laity have been regarded for centuries as "the dumb sheep" to be looked after, to be cared for in a patronizing manner — the implication being that God was not close to *them*. Thankfully, the reforms of Vatican II made serious efforts to bring the laity back into the heart of church life.

Since Vatican II, though, we still find many good people in fear and deep concern about meeting their God in death. Why is it that the church has produced in so many people's minds an image of a God to be feared? The answer might well be found in a failure to keep the focus firmly on Jesus' teaching about God.

Slow to Believe

Jesus had enormous difficulty convincing people to believe in the God in which he believed. At the beginning of his ministry it must have seemed to him that people would readily believe the Good News he bore. We can imagine how enthusiastic he must have been. The blind would see, the lame would walk, the deaf would hear, the dumb would speak, and the poor would have the Good News preached to them! God would be doing great things through him! But very quickly Jesus learned that it was not so easy to get people to embrace Good News. There were more important issues in their lives: the Roman occupation, the keeping of the Law, control over people's religious practice, the protection of one's riches and power, or the long, long religious tradition that should not be questioned —

especially by a prophet from Galilee. Even his own followers were slow to believe and showed that their belief was rather feeble when testing times came.

We can think that none of this affected Jesus very much. Yet he must have been frustrated and weary; he must have worried. He certainly sought inspiration in prayer. He must have searched for solutions and looked for new ways to convince people. He deliberated very carefully before making decisions, for example, spending all night in prayer and reflection before naming the twelve apostles (Luke 6:12).

Jesus, Man of Faith

Surely there were times in his ministry when Jesus' faith in what he believed about God and about himself was tested by the circumstances of his life. He invites us to learn from his experience, to know him in his humanness. These consoling words in Matthew's Gospel are very much linked with sharing human experience:

> Come to me.... Shoulder my yoke and learn from me, for I am gentle and humble in heart, and you will find rest for your souls. Yes my yoke is easy and my burden light. (Matt. 11:28)

The burden is always lighter when we have a friend to share it with. Realizing that Jesus, too, lived by faith will help us know him better and feel closer to him as friend and companion.

The letter to the Hebrews (12:1–6) urges us to keep our eyes on Jesus "who leads us in our faith." In his passion and death experience this faith is put to its greatest test. Jesus had proclaimed the goodness of God. There is a human experience here with which we are all familiar: it is easy enough to believe in God's goodness when all is going well. What happens, though, when all crumbles around us? In these circumstances can we still proclaim that God is good, loving, and faithful? In his time of passion Jesus had all the helps to faith and trust stripped from him. He had been betrayed, rejected, abandoned, left without the support of friends or the comfort of success. He had clearly failed in what he set out to do. He underwent extraordinary physical suffering. Even God seemed to have deserted him. It was as if the circumstances of life turned everything against him. In the depths of that dark abyss where everything screamed it was madness to believe that God is good, faithful, and will come, it was then that Jesus clung to his belief in a loving God.

The Passion

When thinking about Jesus in his passion it becomes particularly necessary to guard against suggestions that it was easy for him "because he is God." It is important that we keep our gaze firmly on the reality of a human person being crucified and on the faith to which this man held. This was not play-acting. Here was a man holding on to his beliefs about God in the midst of darkness and the temptation to despair.

When the circumstances of our lives treat us harshly, it would surely help us if we had a relationship with Jesus, who knew what it was like to have to "trust, endure, and not give up" (1 Cor. 13:7). We need the reassurance that this was a painful struggle for him also. The Good News he brings to us, then, is not only his message about God always with us, but himself also as a friend and companion for us.

It is regrettable that so many Catholics are fearful of entering into the reality of Jesus' humanity because they are afraid of denying his divinity. St. Teresa of Avila has sound advice for us:

> When we are busy, or suffering persecutions, or trials, when we cannot get as much quiet as we should like, and at seasons of aridity, we have a very good friend in Christ. We look at him as a Man; we think of the moments of weakness and times of trial: and He becomes our Companion.[3]

Jesus, Companion and Friend

If we want to develop a worthwhile relationship with Jesus we have to do our part to develop the friendship. It can happen in the same way we develop any friendship — by spending time together and sharing life's experiences.

There is a two-way process in this. On the one hand we have to make the effort to get "inside" Jesus, that is, let him be human and try to see his world and what happens to him from his viewpoint. This involves thinking about his feelings, hopes, dreams, joys, disappointments, hurts, and all the other realities that deeply touched his human heart. Allowing Jesus to be human will deepen our appreciation of the fact that he knows what it is like to walk in our shoes. That will help the other side of the process — our sharing of what happens in our lives with him. Our sharing will be with a Jesus who understands, but who will also challenge us to keep on being faithful to what we believe.

If we do not develop this friendship with Jesus, our Christian experience will lack a heart. The practice of our religion might well be sincere and obedient, but its focus is meant to be on how Jesus and his message set us free from thought patterns and religious practices that enslave us to thinking that God is not near to us. Sharing our lived experience with a Jesus who understands could well be the key to overcoming that "serious error of our age" that Vatican II named: the split between our professed faith and our daily lives.

The Problem of Suffering

It is in the face of tragedy and suffering that our relationship with Jesus and with God is most tested.

Catholics often seek to console someone in times of tragedy with the expression, "Well, it is God's will, and we just have to accept it." And often the person in the midst of the tragedy is left to ask how on earth can a good and loving God take away a young husband or wife, or cripple a spouse for life, or intend whatever the tragedy might be.

Do we believe in a God "somewhere up there" who pulls strings like a puppeteer and who effectively decides that Tom will get killed in an accident one minute and Mandy's baby will be born with a severe heart deformity the next?

We might never find answers to tragedy and suffering and how they connect with a loving God. It may help, however, to consider such issues in the light of Jesus' experience of suffering and tragedy.

Jesus was human as we are. To be human is a risk. It is to be subject to an imperfect way of existing. In this imperfect world we are subject to the imperfections of nature and the choices of other people. Things can and do go wrong. Jesus experienced the pain of things going terribly wrong. In this pain Jesus was *faithful* to his fundamental belief that God is good and loving no matter what the imperfection of the world and his life situation did to him. What life, love, and belief in everything he had preached asked of Jesus was that he keep faith in his God in the midst of suffering. It is this faith of Jesus, severely tested by the human condition, that gives us hope and meaning and sets us free from despair.

Yet it is a commonly held belief that God *wanted* or *willed* Jesus to suffer. What sort of "Father" would want to put a beloved son through suffering and tragedy? Would any parents do that to their child? Why, then, do some people think of God as planning or willing suffering for Jesus — or for any of us?

Jesus, in being faithful, challenges us to have such a strong faith in God's goodness that it will not disappear when life treats us badly. He does this, not by patting us on the head and giving advice, but by living out in his own life the extreme pain of this faith. He has experienced what we sometimes experience in time of great suffering: that faith can seem like a giant leap into darkness. Jesus did not believe in a cruel God, even though life was cruel to him. His teaching and the manner of his living and dying challenge us to rid ourselves of ideas and practices that in any way suggest that our God is an unfeeling "string-puller." We need to examine carefully how we sometimes speak about "God's will." We might well find that we are a long way removed from Jesus' idea of God. If only the church, through its ministers, preached Jesus' idea of God and led people to relate with a human Jesus, fewer people might give up their religion in time of tragedy. Rather than blaming God for "willing" the tragedy and turning their backs on a God they have been led to think of as cruel, they might find some comfort in knowing that Jesus relates to their pain.

Whether we are in pain or not, we are called, as Christians, to have a worthwhile relationship with Jesus, *human* and divine. The mystery is that both are in the same person. We do not solve the mystery by allowing the divinity to drown out the reality of his humanness. Rather, by respecting both the human and the divine realities in Jesus we might be led to discover better that we, too, are a splendid mixture of the human and the divine. Our humanness is not something to be despised, is not inherently sinful, but is a dwelling place of the Sacred. In our human loving and our efforts to be caring and faithful we can discover, as Jesus did, that the Sacred is intimately close to us and is more loving and caring and faithful than we can ever imagine.

Summary

- Let Jesus be human! "Walk in the man, and you will arrive at God."

- To be human is to be limited.

- Use our own experiences and human emotions as stepping stones to know Jesus better in his humanness.

- The Gospels *work backward*. Their starting point is the Risen Jesus. They are shaped by this faith.

- Jesus urges us to new ways of thinking about God and about ourselves in relationship with God.

- We have to change our attitudes if we are to be open to accepting Jesus' teaching. "The kingdom of God is among you. Change, convert, repent... *in order that you may believe the good news.*"

- The God Jesus believed in is not cruel or manipulative. Jesus urges us to trust a God who is like a most loving parent. Loving parents are not cruel to their children, nor are they unfeeling.

- Jesus' faith was put to the test by the circumstances of his life. His faith in what he believed about God faced the ultimate test — he was ready to die for it.

- "Let us not lose sight of Jesus, who leads us in our faith." (Heb. 12:2)

- God does not *will* us to suffer. Life and love and our relationship with Jesus challenge us to imitate the faith of Jesus when life is difficult.

- In the humanness of Jesus we discover a tremendous source of support, encouragement, and compassion. Our Catholic experience must draw on this better than it has in the past.

- In our own humanness we too can discover what Jesus discovered in his humanness: that God is intimately close to us.

Chapter Three

The Eucharist:
How Close God Really Is!

Before reading this chapter, take a few moments to answer the following three questions.

1. Why is the Eucharist important to you?

2. What do you think we are *doing* whenever we come to Eucharist?

3. Why did the eucharistic liturgy change so much after Vatican II?

I N CHAPTER 2 of the Acts of the Apostles the events of
Pentecost are described. Included is the first Christian
homily, the speech of Peter to the crowd:

> People of Israel,
> listen to what I am going to say.
> Jesus the Nazarene was a man commended to you
>   by God
> by the miracles and portents and signs
> that God worked through him when he was among
>   you, as you all know.
> This man . . . you took and had crucified by men
>   outside the Law.
> You killed him, but God raised him to life,
> freeing him from the pangs of Hades. . . .
>
> God raised this man Jesus to life,
> and all of us are witnesses to that.
> Now raised to the heights by God's right hand,
> he has received from the Father the Holy Spirit who
>   was promised,
> and what you see and hear is the outpouring of that
>   Spirit. . . .
> For this reason the whole house of Israel can be
>   certain

that God has made this Jesus whom you crucified
both Lord and Christ.

Peter's words are very significant for they stress this
man Jesus:

- through whom God worked miracles;

- whom God raised;

- to whom God has now given the fullness of the
  Spirit;

- whom God has made both Lord and Christ.

What is striking when we read these lines is the clear
sense that it is only in the event of the Resurrection that
the followers of Jesus begin to articulate their understanding of how Jesus is "Savior." From this understanding
Christian thinkers throughout the ages developed Christian
doctrine concerning the divinity of Jesus. The Resurrection
and the "outpouring of the Spirit" were the convincing
signs for Peter and the apostles that Jesus was now sharing
in the fullness of God's life. It is in light of the Resurrection and this sharing of God's Spirit that the early
Christians reflected upon and told the stories about Jesus'
life. The stories were colored by their clear belief, revealed
through the outpouring of the Spirit, that "God has made
this Jesus whom you crucified both Lord and Christ." As
stated in the previous chapter, it is important for us to real-
ize this when we read the Gospels. What became clearer
after the Resurrection concerning Jesus' relationship with
God was not so clear *before* it.

The Resurrection

The Resurrection of Jesus and the outpouring of the Spirit radically changed people's lives. Peter's preaching to the people is just one example of this astonishing change. Not only did something wonderful happen to Jesus, as Peter proclaims, but something extraordinary happened to those who were close to him. They experienced Jesus their "Lord" present to them in a way they could never have imagined while he was alive. They experienced in themselves the same Spirit they had seen active in the life of Jesus.

The Acts of the Apostles is the story of this incredible change. Frightened people became bold. Men and women witnessed with extraordinary conviction to the presence of Jesus and God's Spirit among them. Stephen was willing to die for this. Peter cured a lame man "in the name of Jesus Christ the Nazarene." The apostles were ready to face prison and punishment. Paul was converted and became the great missionary figure among the early Christian believers. The same Spirit that had moved in Jesus' life drove them on, encouraging and strengthening them.

St. Paul wrote often about the effect that the Resurrection and the sharing of the Spirit are meant to have on Christians. He believed that Christians became a "new creation" because of their closeness with the risen Jesus and through sharing his Spirit. In the following selection from his writings we can sense both the experience and the deep conviction that Paul wanted all Christians to share:

The mystery
is Christ among you,
your hope of glory;
this is the Christ we proclaim,
this is the wisdom
in which we
thoroughly train everyone
and instruct everyone,
to make them all perfect
in Christ.
It is for this
that I struggle wearily on,
helped only by his power,
driving me irresistibly.
(Col. 1:27–29)

And for anyone
who is in Christ,
there is a new creation;
the old creation has gone,
and now the new one is here.
It is all God's work.
It was God who reconciled us
to himself through Christ
and gave us the work
of handing on
this reconciliation.
(2 Cor. 5:17–18)

I live now
not with my own life
but with the life of Christ
who lives in me.
(Gal. 2:20)

...may Christ live
in your hearts
through faith....
Glory be to him
whose power at work in us
can do far more
than we can ask or imagine.
(Eph. 3:17, 20)

In fact, Paul made the belief in Jesus' closeness the test for being a Christian:

> Examine yourselves
> to make sure you are in the faith;
> test yourselves.
> Do you acknowledge
> that Jesus Christ is really in you?
> If not, you have failed the test.
>
> (2 Cor. 13:5)

Religion

The conviction that they shared the same Spirit that moved in Jesus, together with their eventual understanding of Jesus' insights, gave early Christians their answers to the deepest religious questions:

- Where do we find the sacred?
- What is the nature of the sacred?
- How should we relate with it?
- What does it expect of us?
- What is the meaning and purpose of life?

Magic and superstition, law and ritual, "holy people" who know the inner secrets and who have special access — these have played an important part in all religious thinking and practice. Awareness that we all share the Spirit that moved Jesus fulfills this religious search and prompts us to answer these questions in a radically new way:

- God is beyond imagining, yet our God is intimately close to us.
- Our God is good and loving.
- Loving our neighbor is the greatest expression of love for our God.
- In loving we will find our meaning and purpose in life.
- We are to approach our God with trust and gratitude, free from fear.

This is good news that demands to be shared with the whole world!

Early Christians

The early Christians were conscious that the presence of God's Spirit within and among them was pure gift. They did not win the gift. They did not deserve it. The fact it was pure gift expanded their hearts and minds. It was the experience of a God who loved them so freely. Their understanding was expressed in these words:

> God loved us with so much love
> that he was generous with his mercy:
> when we were dead through our sins,
> he brought us to life with Christ....
> This was to show for all ages to come,
> through his goodness toward us in Christ Jesus,
> how infinitely rich he is in grace.
> Because it is by grace that you have been saved,
>   through faith;
> not by anything of your own,
> but by a gift from God. (Eph. 2:4–7)

Something radically new happened as a result of their awareness of sharing God's Spirit. The text above from Ephesians reflects their awareness that this was God's gift to them, not something they had earned by their own efforts. We think we understand this today, yet our religious practices and attitudes are often tainted with the belief that *we* have to make the effort to get to God. We find it difficult to believe what the early Christians believed:

- We are "Temples of God's Spirit" (see 1 Cor. 3:16).

- We are children of God (see 1 John 3:1).

We are, then, sacred places; the sacred dwells within us.

The Eucharist

At the center of this Good News that we call the Gospel is Jesus, the man who revealed God to us in such a beautiful way. He is the Risen Lord, the Savior wanting to set us free from images and thoughts about God that would constrain and bind us into fear, distrust, and superstition. Through him, with him, and in him we join together to give praise and thanks to God. Our best means of doing this is in the Eucharist.

The Early Centuries

When the early Christians came together for Eucharist, they brought this Christ-centered awareness of themselves to their gatherings. The Eucharist put them in touch again and again with the presence of Jesus. It imaged again and again who they were: the bread taken and blessed. They came to the Eucharist aware that they were bearers of the sacred. One of the early bishops in our church, St. Ignatius of Antioch, spoke of the Eucharist as "the source and the image of the Christian life."

The Eucharist proclaimed and celebrated the marvelous things God had done through Jesus. It was very much a community celebration. It focused strongly on the community as "the Body" of Christ, with both the privilege and the responsibility that accompany this truth. The Christians knew they were privileged; they also knew they had the responsibility of loving one another as Jesus loved them. They knew they were called to continue the mission of Jesus in the world. They knew their "Amen" response to "The Body of Christ" at communion time was their commitment *to be* the Body of Christ for one another.

In the early centuries the liturgy usually took place in a home. The gathering was not large. It would have been a close-knit group of people, well known to each other. The presider was usually the leader of the community, a married man in most cases. People were there through personal choice, often at great personal risk. We need to understand that this gathering gave meaning to their lives. These people felt very close to Jesus and to one another. It was the way they loved one another that attracted others to the community. The care and concern for one another, especially the poor, were a particular focus of the liturgy through their prayers, their gestures (the sign of peace), and the gifts *everyone* brought for distribution.

It is important for us to understand that the people were not present at the Eucharistic liturgy as spectators. Since liturgy imaged for them that they were "the Body of Christ," they participated accordingly, as one body. They did so through their responses, their singing, the offerings for the needy, the prayers for the church community, the sign of peace for one another, and the way they shared in the meal. They clearly understood that being at the Eucharist challenged them to share their lives with one another as Jesus did.

The Eucharist Begins to Change

An enormous change to this close-knit, supportive liturgy came in the fourth century following the conversion of Constantine, when Christianity became the official religion of the Roman Empire. As a result there was a sudden and huge increase in the number of Christians. There was now little risk and less personal choice attached to being Christian. This caused a corresponding lessening in commitment, a watering down of conversion, and a weakening of the challenge to be seen as different. The overall effect was a diluted Christianity: many people were "Christian" in name only.

A clear result of these changes was the loss of the voice of the laity in decision making. No longer was the Christian community a close-knit group of people working together, each conscious of the gifts he or she brought to the life of the community. The changes involved a shift from small, intimate communities, in which all participated, to large communities of whole villages or towns. The setting for liturgy moved into a larger space — like the town hall that was called the basilica. The great increase in numbers, along with the weakening of commitment, made it no longer possible for the whole community to be involved in decision making. Both the civil and the religious community now came to center around the bishop, who found himself busy with many administrative matters.

The rapid spread of Christianity led to the bishop designating priests to represent him at any celebrations of the Eucharist he could not attend. This was a new development in the church, and it set a new pattern for authority in the church: the bishop at a distance from his people.

The Middle Ages

The eighth to the eleventh centuries had a profound and lasting effect on the eucharistic liturgy. For some of this period leadership from the popes was often weak and ineffective. Some of them rarely presided at liturgies and gave scandal when they did. The Arian heresy, which taught that Jesus was only human, brought a reaction so emphasizing the divinity of Jesus that it became dangerous to speak of Jesus as human. As a result, teaching and preaching distanced Jesus from our human experience. Coupled with several centuries of teaching that the body was basically sinful, this helped to develop the sense of distance between God and the Christian faithful. The divine and the human were well and truly separated.

Unworthiness

It was inevitable with this background that a theology of unworthiness flourished. The early Christians had been led to a sense of God's extraordinary love, as in Paul's statement, "We are the earthenware jars that hold a treasure."

In these centuries people were led to see only the cracks in the jars — they could not possibly be homes to the sacred. The focus was on sin, failure, and unworthiness. Christians learned to fear God and became very conscious of their distance from God. In the eleventh century several well-known writers considered that only monks had a good chance of getting to heaven. Preaching on hell, purgatory, and the fear of judgment flourished.

There is a healthy theology of unworthiness, and there is also an unhealthy one.

A healthy theology says, in effect,

We are sinners.
We do not deserve God's love and God's presence.
But look at the marvelous things God has done for us!

An unhealthy theology says,

We are sinners.
We do not deserve God's love and God's presence.
Therefore, God could not be close to the likes of us.

Such an unhealthy theology of unworthiness has had a long-lasting impact in the church.

More Changes in the Eucharist

Hand in hand with the preaching of unworthiness went a theology of the Eucharist that the early Christians would never have recognized or accepted in their intimate home settings. This theology stressed the awesome "great mystery." The "Mass" became the great sacred drama. The fact that people did not speak or understand Latin added to the sense of mystery. The focus shifted from the "God-with-us," the God near to us in our human imperfections, to the God remote from us, the God to be feared.

Masses celebrated by the priest alone became common at this time. This growth in private Masses had its effect: silence became important. By the year 1000 the priest was obliged to say the Canon of the Mass in a whisper. It was surrounded with mystery and silence.

There were other long-lasting effects:

- People were preoccupied with mystery.

- There was an exaggerated reverence of objects.

- Prayers emphasized unworthiness.

- "I" prayers were used by the priest rather than "We" prayers.

- Communion rails highlighted the distance between the people and the sacred place.

- The priest celebrated Mass with his back to the people.

- Most laity stopped going to communion because they thought they were unworthy. (In 1215, the Fourth Lateran Council had to pass a law to make people go at least once a year!)

- If people came to communion, they had to kneel to receive.

- The Blessed Sacrament was reserved for adoration and processions.

- The tabernacle became the focal point of Catholic piety. It was seen as the place where the sacred was situated.

- Genuflecting to sacred things and places, especially the tabernacle, reenforced the concept that the sacred was to be found there *rather than* in the people themselves.

It is obviously very important to reverence the eucharistic bread. It is very sacred to us. But to think that the sacred dwells *only* in the consecrated bread would be wrong. This is a long way removed from early Christian belief and practice, which stressed that the people themselves are "temples of God's Spirit," the "Body of Christ." Once that belief is lost sight of, as it clearly was in these centuries, liturgy simply perpetuates a misunderstanding of basic Christian belief. The people become the "have-nots," the unredeemed crowd, at a distance from their God. This sense of distance from God has permeated Christianity for centuries.

Role of the Laity at Eucharist

Now, although their role in the Eucharistic liturgy (by then commonly called the Mass) had become almost totally passive, people still tried to make sense of the sacred drama. They gave meanings to gestures and signs that were now foreign to them. Often the meaning was connected to the passion of Jesus, e.g., three signs of the cross close together in the canon symbolized the three times Jesus was mocked; the five times the priest turned to the people symbolized five appearances of the risen Jesus; three moments of special silence symbolized the three days Jesus spent in the tomb.

The elevation of the Host after the consecration then became the high point of the Mass for the laity. This became linked with mystery and superstition. Joseph Powers, S.J., gives a clear picture of what the Mass had become in the eleventh century:

> Thus a Eucharistic piety developed which was almost totally foreign to the Roman Mass of the fourth and fifth centuries. In those times, the community itself was the focus of the celebration, this to the extent that in the liturgy of the Roman basilica, the altar itself was only a table brought into the presbyterium when it came time for the Eucharistic prayers and offerings. Now the altar became a stage on which a sacred drama took place and the function of the congregation was that of observing the sacred action. Indeed, the Eucharistic piety of the eleventh century and later consisted primarily in gazing on the elevated Host, the act of adoration which was the source of most of the "fruits" of the Mass. And these "fruits" as they are presented in some of the more popular devotional treatments are quite remarkable: one does not grow older while one attends Mass; the souls in purgatory do not suffer while one offers Mass for them; a woman who gives birth on the day she attends Mass will have a son. It is no great wonder that the

faithful moved from altar to altar in the great churches to see the elevation. Fortescue tells of the cries of the English which were heard if the Host was not elevated high enough: "Hold up, Sir John, hold up. Heave it a little higher!"[4]

People at a Distance from God

The key elements in Eucharistic piety that were to last for centuries (and that still have an effect) became: "Keep your distance!" "Look and adore!" "Don't touch!" The "Eucharist" had become an object, a thing, most sacred, rather than the activity of a community celebrating God's presence with them. Eucharistic piety centered on the tabernacle rather than on the presence of God within and among God's people. As a result, the major questions in Eucharistic theology centered on how Jesus was present in the consecrated bread and wine. Eucharistic practice became tied to ritual: making all the gestures exactly as laid down by liturgical law. In fact, from 1570 onward nothing could be changed, not a word, not a gesture. The Sacred Congregation of Rites came into existence in the sixteenth century for the express purpose of being watchdog to such rigidity. In the Catholic Church, law and rubrics continued to dominate liturgical practice until the Second Vatican Council.

Magic, superstition, an emphasis on law and ritual, select "holy people" with secrets and special access to the sacred, the "faithful" fearful of their God and conscious of their distance from God....*Is this what Jesus intended?* Is this what should characterize the gathering of the "Body of Christ"? Is this what the radical new beginning ushered in at Pentecost sought to achieve?

Vatican II Renewal

The renewal movement begun in Vatican II emphasized a return to the sources of Christianity, especially to Scripture and to early church practice. Vatican II was not concerned with change just for the sake of change. The prime concern was renewing our awareness of ourselves as "the People of God," as sharers of the Spirit. It was inevitable that in regaining the sense of ourselves as a people close to God there would be major changes in the way we worship. Liturgy would need to give witness to the truth that we gather as a "body," not just as separate individuals. It would need to express that God is near to us, and that the Spirit's gifts of ministry belong to the community, to all who are baptized and not just to ordained males.

Most of the liturgical changes we have experienced are not new to the church. Communion in the hand, drinking from the chalice, the words used at communion ("The Body of Christ. Amen"), the offertory procession, the Prayers of the Faithful, these were all once part of our Roman rites. Through the renewal the church has been trying to lead us to the awareness, very strong in the sources of our tradition, of the presence of God's Spirit within and among us. Without taking anything away from the sacredness of the consecrated bread and wine, we have been asked to focus more than we had in recent centuries on our responsibility to *be* the Body of Christ. Now we are called to recapture the early tradition of our church that Eucharist is something we *do.* It is an action that expresses the reality of who we are — people who commit ourselves to making evident in our world the Spirit that Jesus made evident in his life. The Second Vatican Council's Constitution on the Liturgy urges priests, *as a matter of duty*, to ensure that the Eucharist is celebrated with this renewed emphasis on the active, knowledgeable, and fruitful participation of the faithful:

> Pastors of souls must therefore realize that, when the liturgy is celebrated, *more is required than the mere observance of the laws governing valid and licit celebration.* It is their duty also to ensure that the faithful take part knowingly, actively, and fruitfully.[5] (Emphasis added)

The Challenge

What we must seek to create is liturgy that expresses clearly and strongly that the Spirit that moved in Jesus' life is among us and that we are the Body of Christ. This is the purpose behind the changes. Yet it is surprising how little attention is paid to this fact. When liturgical changes are made without seeking to deepen the people's understanding of themselves as people close to God, the changes cause confusion and even hurt. In other words, if present liturgical change is simply placed alongside a mentality of "Life as a Journey *to* God," then it will not achieve its purpose. The changes have to be accompanied by an understanding of ourselves as people close to God, sharers of the same Spirit that moved in the life of Jesus. With this understanding we will appreciate better what it means to call ourselves "church."

Summary

- It is only in the Resurrection that an understanding of the divinity of Jesus is articulated.

- The "outpouring of the Spirit" was the convincing sign that Jesus had been "raised to the heights by God's right hand."

- The Resurrection changed the lives of ordinary people. They experienced the presence of the Spirit that had moved so visibly in Jesus' life in and among them.

- "I live now with the life of Christ who lives in me." (Col. 2:20)

- The Spirit is God's gift. We do not earn it.

- In the Eucharistic liturgy the early Christians celebrated the experience of being "temples of God's Holy Spirit," "the Body of Christ," and ritualized their acceptance of the responsibility that went with this experience.

- They *participated* accordingly in the Eucharist.

- A change occurred from small communities with participation and choice to very large communities.

- An unhealthy theology of worthiness developed. God cannot be close to us!

- Liturgy then expressed distance from God in many ways.

- With distance came fear, with a focus on damnation and purgatory.

- People became passive spectators at Mass. Keep your distance; look and adore. There was a growth of superstitious practices.

- The sacred was found not in people, but in things.

- Vatican II renewal is not about change for the sake of change. It is based on a return to our early tradition and the truth that we are all bearers of God's Spirit.

Chapter Four

The Church: Called to Be Witnesses of God's Presence

Before reading this chapter you might like to spend a few moments considering the following questions:

1. Who or what has helped you in recent years to develop your appreciation of your faith?

2. What does belonging to a "church" mean for you personally?

3. On a scale of one to ten,

   • How would you score your parish in terms of taking seriously lay involvement and lay responsibility?

   • How would you score your parish liturgy in terms of its being uplifting, affirming, encouraging, and challenging?

T HE PROCESS OF RENEWAL in the Catholic Church has not been smooth or easy. The process faced the task of changing some attitudes and practices that had become part of Catholic life over the past thousand years. In fact, some of these practices and attitudes were realities by which Catholics identified themselves, for example, the Latin Mass and not eating meat on Fridays.

For many people it seemed the changes just suddenly happened, but it was not like that. Many years of study and research led to the reforms of the Second Vatican Council. To give an appreciation of this we will look briefly at the work of just one person, Yves Congar, a French Dominican priest.

In the 1930s Congar and some of his friends conducted an investigation into "causes of unbelief" in the church. In his summary of the results of the investigation, Congar wrote:

> It was clear to me that, insofar as it depended on us, the cause of unbelief was largely related to a poor presentation of the church, to a not very attractive, even repulsive appearance, one that was wholly juridico-hierarchical. Something would have to change.[6]

In simple terms, "juridico-hierarchical" means: organized according to law and structure, with power concentrated at the top. This structure is like a pyramid in which those at the bottom have nothing to give to those above them. The role of those at the bottom is to receive and obey.

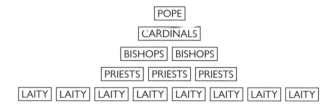

This model of being church has existed for many centuries. It is certainly familiar to Catholics, and there are advantages in seeing the church this way. Authority is clear and definite, with a strong emphasis on tradition and the teaching role of those at the top. It is a clear point of reference for the whole church.

There are, however, aspects that contribute to the "poor presentation" to which Congar and his friends refer. These are evident whenever:

- The manner of teaching tends to talk down to people.

- Those in authority do not consult.

- There is a presumption that only those in positions of authority are blessed with the Spirit of Truth.

- The language used is too difficult to be understood by the vast majority of people.

- There is an emphasis on uniformity, to the extent that the church becomes "Roman" in widely differing cultures.

- Enormous energy is spent on being watchdog over the worldwide acceptance of Roman law, power, and ways of thinking.

Such a church can often seem out of touch with the lived experience of ordinary people. An unfortunate consequence is that many people who hold positions of authority seem unwilling to trust the movement of God's Spirit in people today. Their model of being church seems to maintain what Pope Pius X wrote back in 1906:

> The church is an unequal society. . . . As far as the multitude is concerned, they have no other duty than to let themselves be led. (*Vehementer Nos* no. 8)

Was This Always Our Tradition?

Congar's special field of study had been the early centuries of the church's history. Seeking the change that was needed, Congar looked to the beginnings of our Christian tradition — "Scripture, the fathers, the liturgy, the great councils, and the very life of the church, the Christian community."[7] It is important that we appreciate how the renewal movement in the church has been grounded in these traditional sources. People who fail to understand this often become confused by "all the changes." They wonder why we have to have so many and lament them as being unfaithful to our tradition. A poor welcome and response is then given to the Spirit's work of vitality and renewal among us.

In 1941 Congar wrote of the church as "Mystery." This may seem innocent enough to us today, but at the time the

Roman church authorities became suspicious of his ideas because they challenged the way they had come to view the church. Seeing the church as a "mystery" seemed to question the structural organization that had been in place for centuries: the juridico-hierarchical model of church.

Congar, using the sources mentioned earlier, wrote of the church in a very different way. He wrote about a Spirit-filled "body" on a journey. He described the church as a "communio" — a union of people with God. This was seen in our previous chapter in the description of the early church communities as close-knit, supportive communities. Then, there was an awareness that people were bound together by the action of the Holy Spirit, and that the gifts of the Spirit were given to every member of the community. Authority in such a community was not a matter of one person lording it over others, or of decisions being handed down to people who had no say in the decision making.

Any office of authority was not "from above," but from among, within, the community.

People gathered around leader

Authority . . . the Real Issue?

The communion model of church stresses the importance of authority. It insists on the need for authority and order.

But it also recognizes that people should be involved and that authority should help people grow and develop. True authority assures people that they have been heard and taken seriously. For a long time in the church the model of authority has been:

- I teach,
- You listen,
- You obey.

But Congar insisted that the early church tradition of authority was rather:

- We listen,
- I learn,
- I teach.

Congar had an enormous influence on how we think about the laity. For him, the laity certainly did not belong at the bottom of a pyramid. It is clear from the early centuries that the laity are not second-class citizens in the church. They *are* the community. They share the gifts of the Spirit for the building up of the community. Their participation in the Eucharistic celebration must be active and vibrant. So Congar wrote at length on "the priesthood of the laity" and the laity's rightful place in the church as sharers of God's Spirit.

We take much of this for granted today. Congar, how-ever, was not thanked for his enormous contribution prior to the Second Vatican Council. Instead, he was held under suspicion by Rome. He and other writers who laid the theo-logical foundations for the Council were closely watched.

Their academic activity was frequently restricted, and they themselves were sometimes silenced by Roman authorities. Their works were carefully inspected and criticized. Congar himself was virtually exiled from his own country for some years. Many of his own Dominican brothers disagreed with him. It wasn't until the Council that he and other writers received due recognition for their contributions.

The opposition to Congar and other theologians undoubtedly arose because of the enormous consequences of what they were saying. If they were right, then the church would have to change quite dramatically. For a church that prided itself on not changing, this was threatening and unsettling, a time of great risk.

It was not that change in itself was so threatening. It was the *nature* of the change. If Congar was right, then the pyramid model would need drastic review. It would now need to take into account the truth that the laity are Spirit-filled people. It would need to acknowledge their rightful place in the church and change from viewing the laity as listeners, obeyers, and passive spectators in the church's sacramental life. They are not there simply as a group to be ministered to by the clergy. They are a people empowered by baptism and the presence of the Spirit. They, too, are called to minister in some ways to each other and, in fact, be the church in the world.

On a wider scene, the remodeling would need to take into account the presence and activity of God in other religions and other cultures. The Catholic Church would no longer be able to view itself as the sole possessor of Truth. It could no longer teach, for example, the following:

The holy Roman church firmly believes, professes and proclaims that none of those who are outside the Catholic Church — not only pagans, but Jews also, heretics and schismatics — can have part in eternal life, but will go into eternal fire, unless they are gathered into that church before the end of life. (Pope Eugene at the end of the Council of Florence in 1442; see the official documents of the Council of Florence.)

The Task of Leadership

Vatican II shaped the remodeling. It has not been easy, and the path ahead will not be easy. It has not been an easy task to move Catholics to a rightful sense of themselves as people gifted and empowered by the Spirit of God. It is certain that the remodeling will fail unless Catholics continue to be led to this truth about themselves and to accept the responsibility that comes with it. This must surely be one of the main tasks of leadership in the church today, yet the lament for the lack of this kind of leadership is loud. On the other hand, lament comes also from those leaders who are trying to lead Catholics to this deeper sense of themselves. They are frequently frustrated by the attitude of many who are in and out of Sunday Eucharist as if it were a service station: they do not want to get involved.

What Does It Mean to Be "Church"?

The early Christians would have found it difficult to comprehend that people could consider that they belonged to the "church" and not witness to it through their lifestyle and sharing in the community's worship. For them, to be in the "church" meant active participation. It meant an openness to the Word of God, the desire to follow Jesus, a willingness to be bonded with other people who gathered to listen, to praise, to celebrate, and who tried to witness to the Good News through their lifestyle. Passive, noninvolved membership would have contradicted their understanding of being Christian.

Some of this passivity and noninvolvement may be caused by a lack of interest. But there is another side to the passivity that is evident even among those who consider themselves regular and faithful churchgoers. Karl Rahner, S.J., one of the most respected theologians of the twentieth century, named it "lifelessness." He wrote, "If we are honest, we must admit that we are to a terrifying extent a spiritually lifeless Church."[8]

How is this lifelessness evident?

- When we accept answers handed to us from others.

- When we will not make the effort as adults to question and make our faith something personal.

- When we let ritualism and boredom dominate our liturgy.

- When we refuse to allow ourselves to be challenged seriously by the Gospel to reach out to others.

- When we see membership in the church as something passive instead of as a strong commitment to be disciples of Jesus.

• When we allow the Word of God to be badly proclaimed and poorly heard.

Our church, our parish community, will have life to the extent that we are willing to engage in a strong relationship with Jesus, to hear his call and follow him. That is our primary task as Christians. It is a personal task that no one else can do for any of us. Rahner expressed the conviction that the failure in the church's public life can be traced to the failure to proclaim Jesus vigorously. He was convinced that church talk about God and Jesus lacks vitality. The church's public life, he wrote, does not address the lived experience of people, nor the lived experience of Jesus, nor our engagement with the challenge of the Gospel. Rather it "is dominated to a terrifying extent by ritualism, legalism, administration, and a boring and resigned mediocrity along familiar lines."[9]

This will change, he says, only when Christians are willing to develop a personal understanding of their faith:

> Our present situation is one of transition . . . to a Church made up of those who have struggled with their environment in order to reach a personally clear and explicitly responsible decision of faith. This will be the Church of the future or there will be no Church at all.[10]

If he is right, then we should be asking if we have that personal understanding of our faith, whether we are being led to it, and whether we are ourselves doing anything to increase our understanding beyond what we learned in our school days. In other words, we are called as Christians not to live "answers" given to us, no matter how good those answers may be, but to reach into our own hearts and experience and there to engage the questions of faith as adults. We may well come to the same conclusions and we will appreciate the teaching available to us, but the effort will help our faith to be a "personally clear and explicitly responsible decision of faith." We will then belong to the church as a result of an adult decision, not simply because we were born into it. Important in that adult decision will be the issues covered in these chapters:

- How I see myself in relation with God.

- My relationship with Jesus, human and divine.

- How I see myself in relationship with others with whom I am bonded through Jesus and the Spirit.

Unfortunately, such questioning and personal searching is not always met with appreciation within the church. Some people cannot quite see the need for it and are ready to condemn the searchers. They point to church teaching and tradition as if we have there a package of truths that need only to be opened if we wish to discover the answers. The searching seems to be an attack on authority or disloyalty to the church. Some of the condemnation is evident in the powerful and strong pressure being exerted at all levels of church life today against change and renewal. Part of it is a fear that things will get out of control; part of it is a need for security.

Part of it is the in-bred Catholic attitude that implies that we should not question anything that "Rome" says.

Too often today the burning question in the church is that of obedience to Rome. While we must recognize the need to safeguard our sacred tradition, it does seem at times that the question of vigorously proclaiming the Gospel of Jesus comes second. Yet no doctrine is more important than being ready to give one's heart and soul to the message of Jesus. This is not to downplay doctrine, for our doctrine is vitally important to us. It seems, though, that there is a common tendency to equate being a good Catholic with either knowing the doctrine or being willing to hold up one's hand and affirm that one is willing to give assent to whatever the pope says.

Being a good Catholic rests, rather, on one's willingness to be a close disciple of Jesus. Who he is for each of us must be far more important than being able to give answers *about* him. Doctrine and authority have their place within the church, helping us to this personal faith in Jesus. They should never become an end in themselves or become *the* testing point of what makes a good Catholic. The church is not an end in itself. It exists to call us to the story of Jesus and to help us celebrate the reality of God's Spirit in our lives. If it is not doing that, either on a parish or a global level, then the church is failing.

The Parish

We are all called to be the church and to live that reality. This means that on the parish level parishioners must come to an understanding that they are responsible for this reality called "church." This will not happen without preaching and instruction that leads them to an awareness of their call to holiness and the presence of God's Spirit with them in all they do.

Parishioners must then be allowed to *be* church. We must go beyond the lip service that says to parishioners, "This is your parish," but which, in effect, has meant they are expected to do the work without the accompanying responsibility.

Allowing parishioners to be church will bring a change to our thinking about ministry. It is not a matter of helping the priest, nor is it a matter of any priest dealing out a share in his ministry when parishioners take communion to the sick, visit the infirm, proclaim the Word of God, or engage in other ministries that are not restricted to ordained ministers. Rather, it is a matter of parishioners having a God-given right through baptism to minister to one another in the name of Jesus, for the building up of the community.

It must be noted, too, that lack of progress is sometimes caused by attitudes and expectations that many parishioners have and will not change. Some parishioners can be very demanding in expecting that their priests will continue to operate as priests did thirty years ago. Many still want "Father" to do the tasks that should belong to the ministry of parishioners. Many still hunger for the decisiveness that was evident in the parish when one man had all the control. It is not unusual today to hear the complaint from some parishioners, "We don't know who is running the parish these days." It is not unusual, either, for those men and women who are willing to accept the challenge and the responsibility of being church as described in these pages to be criticized. They are often accused of forming a "clique." It is not unusual for this accusation to come from people who will not get involved themselves but are ready to use the accusation to justify their lack of involvement. One of the toughest tasks of a priest's role in parish ministry today is that of leading a majority of parishioners to an acceptance of the reality that they are the church in a particular region or suburb, and that they all have to take responsibility for being the church there.

Avery Dulles, S.J., in his book *A Church to Believe In* addresses the difficulty of this task in his first chapter:

> The ineffectiveness of certain apostolates, I suspect, is closely linked with an inability on the part of Catholics to form an image of the Church into which they can plausibly fit what they think they ought to be doing. Some of the current images of the Church are repugnant; others are seemingly unrelated to daily experience. If we could fashion an inspiring and realistic image of the Church, we might be able to act confidently, and in such a way that our self-understanding would be reinforced by feedback from others.

He goes on to say that in the minds of most people, Catholic or non-Catholic,

> the prevailing image of the Catholic Church is highly institutional. The Church is understood in terms of

dogmas, laws, and hierarchical agencies which impose heavy demands of conformity.[11]

It is striking how these words remind us of Congar's phrase in the 1930s: "wholly juridico-hierarchical." Despite the reforms of the Second Vatican Council, we are still grappling with the same problem: our idea of what it is to be church.

Dulles continues,

> To be a good Catholic, according to the popular view, is simply to adhere to the beliefs and practices demanded by the office holders. At the risk of caricature, one may say that many think of the Church as a huge, impersonal machine set over against its own members.[12]

If Congar is right in asserting that unbelief is linked with a poor presentation of the church, then one of our tasks as Catholics will be to change the way we present ourselves as church. This change must start on the parish level as we review the image and reality of ourselves as church. Some of the challenges we face may be listed under the following headings: Adult Faith Development, Preaching, Liturgy, Ministry, Openness, and Respecting Differences.

Adult Faith Development

In adulthood we discover more and more that the faith we developed in our schooldays struggles to cope with

the questions and issues of adult life. The need to pro-
vide opportunities for adults to deepen their understanding
of their faith may be greater now than ever before. For a
long time we had standard answers for most of life's questions and could defend our beliefs, but today there is much
uncertainty.

We look to our parish community, then, and ask:

- What is our parish doing to help us move beyond the
  knowledge of our faith we acquired at school?

- Are we being helped to formulate what our faith
  means to us?

- Are we creating opportunities to share our faith, to
  deepen our belief and our understanding in the light
  of changes in the church?

- Are there opportunities for us to grow in our knowledge and appreciation of Jesus?

- Does our faith relate with our experiences of midlife,
  marital difficulty, divorce, retirement, grief, tragedy,
  fear of death?

- Can we learn how to integrate prayer and our daily
  living better?

- Can our Catholic faith help us to live more whole-
  some, peaceful, meaningful lives?

Dolores Leckey, who had many years' experience as
executive director of the U.S. Bishops Laity Secretariat
summarized the longings of U.S. Catholics in these words:

Fundamentally, we, i.e., you and I, need the same things. We need commitment and community to move ever more deeply into our spiritual depths, to face who we are, who God is, what the world is all about and how we participate in it all, either creatively or negatively. So, first is some kind of authentic, ongoing spiritual development — steady and reliable.[13]

Part of this process is not only for people to share, but also for them to experience that they are being listened to, that the church's ordained ministers hear what they are saying about life and faith.

Small communities or groups within the parish will become more and more important in parish life if faith development is given the attention it deserves. A ten-minute homily on Sunday is no longer sufficient for handling the questions of life and faith. The wider parish scene will not be able to handle the sharing and the listening. These need small groups built on trust, a willingness to listen to one another, and a readiness to reflect on faith and life. In such groups, people may come to a better awareness of God's presence with them in their everyday lives. One writer comments,

People still long for God, even when they don't know what it is they are longing for. . . . And everywhere people who feel this obscure longing get together to find ways to articulate it, to do something about it. . . . These groups have two things in common:

1. They are reacting against the cult of bigness; they are aware that at a certain point, bigness leads to a loss of real contact, and facilitates manipulation rather than co-operation in human life.

2. There is an awareness of the positive value of being in a group small enough for people to relate to each other very directly.

What I perceive in such little, varied and struggling communities is the early stages of the happening called "church."[14]

When parishioners today are asked to list the needs within their parish, adult faith development usually ranks high. In some parishes little happens, even after such consultation. Sometimes this can be blamed on clergy who simply will not give leadership or seem fearful the people might get wrong ideas. Usually, though, it is because clergy and people have yet to recognize that taking adult faith development seriously is demanding work. It requires a new way of thinking about the parish — seeing groups within the parish as a matter of very high priority. It then requires the initiative to invite people to form such groups and the hard work of giving support to them when they do.

Are such groups just optional extras for our parishes? Or are they indispensable for helping adults to bridge the gap between faith and their lived experience? There seems to be plenty of evidence to suggest that they should not be considered an optional extra.

Preaching

If a parish sincerely wants to renew the way it is church, parishioners could begin by noting what type of church is conveyed by the preaching they hear. Likewise priests could ask themselves what image of church they are presenting. They should be open to discussing this with parishioners. Some questions to help the process could be:

- Does the Sunday preaching insistently call us to a personal relationship with Jesus?

- Does it challenge us to true discipleship, at a cost?

- Does it inspire us with a sense of our own value in God's sight?

- Does it encourage and strengthen in us a deeper awareness of God's presence with us?

- Does it urge us to respond with expanded vision to the reality of God's love for us?

- Does it call us beyond the limits we set on ourselves and on our faith?

- Does it relate the Word of God to the reality of our lived experience?

Henri Nouwen, writing about people who can share the movements of their own inner lives, makes this comment on preaching:

In this context preaching means...the careful and sensitive articulation of what is happening in the community so that those who listen can say: "You say what

I suspected, you express what I vaguely felt, you bring to the fore what I fearfully kept at the back of my mind."[15]

Unfortunately, the alternatives to this type of preaching are heard all too frequently:

- preaching that does not disturb our middle-class values;

- preaching that speaks down to us;

- preaching that focuses on our unworthiness to the detriment of the Good News;

- preaching that highlights only the hierarchical notion of the church;

- preaching that never strongly acknowledges that the parishioners are "temples of God's Spirit."

Liturgy

The following questions might help readers assess the quality of their Sunday liturgy:

- Does our Sunday Eucharist consistently affirm God's closeness to us in all we do?

- Does it ritualize our willingness to be "taken, blessed, broken, and given" for the sake of our "neighbor," whoever that may be?

- Is God's Word presented in such a way that it actually touches our hearts and minds and brings Good News to our lived experience?

- Does our sense of bonding in being the Body of Christ flow over into our hospitality toward one another?

- Are the symbols and language meaningful?

The Sunday Eucharist reflects what sort of church we are. Benedictine priest Nathan Mitchell describes what he believes happens all too often:

[Liturgy] is boring and insipid because people are being duped into accepting responsibility without power, ministry without recognition, participation without decision-making, and change without the franchise. The sacred, of its nature, empowers; the sacred raises up and enables. But the liturgy seems to empower no one with anything, except those already in power; it merely invites the participants to return next week and try it again.[16]

Very often it is difficult to see the connection between what we do at the Sunday Eucharist and what Jesus did with his friends at the Last Supper. It is difficult when we notice, for example, that:

- the front seats are left vacant;

- people are sitting apart from one another;

- the reading is poorly proclaimed;

- responses and singing are half-hearted;

- the bread neither looks like nor tastes like bread;

- the chalice is not offered to the people;

- the presider has little eye-contact with the people and his words and gestures do not "include" the congregation.

Liturgy must draw us together. However, we will not be drawn together as long as:

1. There is an overemphasis on ritual and rubric on the part of the priest. When this happens everything is done correctly to the least detail, but the congregation is not engaged in the liturgical action. It may be "nice," "correct," and "beautiful," but it often fails to touch the lived experience of people.

2. There is a service-station mentality: parishioners coming to get their weekly "dose" of God and making little effort to reach out to others.

An interesting observation that emerged from the Notre Dame Study of U.S. parishes and their liturgy is that the tone of the liturgy is set in the first few minutes:

> At one-third of the Masses, the celebrant simply omitted any opening remarks . . . or welcomed the faithful to participate in the Mass and slipped quickly into the penitential rite. The data indicate that this omission is associated with poor rapport between parishioners and presiding celebrant, diminished community awareness, and poor congregational participation.[17]

Ministry

Ministry should develop from the reality that the Spirit of God blesses all the baptized with gifts, and that sometime, somewhere, in some way, a baptized person should use those gifts in a public manner for the good of the community — especially when the community issues an invitation to do so. This means we have to take seriously the presence of the Spirit among us and allow the Spirit's life, vision, and creativity to move among us. Discernment will always be necessary, and so will risk and trust. Some pertinent questions for a parish community to reflect on could be:

- Is ours a parish that is seen to be taking that risk through the way parishioners are encouraged to let the Spirit lead them?

- Do we have a sense that we *are* the church in the world?

- Do we have a sense that the Spirit is alive and working through the people in our parish?

In those parishes where the hierarchical, clerical model of church is in operation, the priest has control and sees the role of parishioners characterized by obedience and submission to him. People may well be called upon for help, but they will clearly remain "helpers." The parish may be run efficiently — this is one benefit of tight control — but it might well be achieved at the cost of the parishioners' baptismal rights to ministry. People who like someone to make the decisions for them appreciate this style of leadership.

Openness

The parish community cannot remain inward-looking if it is truly to be church. The church is of its nature missionary, spreading the Gospel, calling others to follow Jesus. We do not seem to do this well in our middle-class parishes. We are more likely to let a group in the parish look after the RCIA rather than accept the truth that each parishioner has a responsibility to invite or attract others to the faith. If our parish is not attracting new members, whose fault is it? The answer is: the fault of each one of us, if we believe that we have something worthwhile to offer as a parish community.

We have to accept some responsibility also for issues of concern in our church and in our world. We do not exist as a church in order to take comfort in Jesus' love for us. To love as he loved and to look at our church, our society, our world, with his eyes is to be challenged to move beyond using the church as a comfort station. For example, how would Jesus listen to a woman concerned about women's issues in the church?

Many parishes seem unable to bring such issues to parishioners' awareness. One way of doing this would be to ensure that the parish has a social justice committee. Part of the role of this group would be to bring issues of concern and justice to the attention of parishioners. We are largely uninformed about issues of social justice, yet we are expected to voice opinions. Many of the issues seem too complex for us to understand. On some we hear no comment from church leaders (although on the other side, how often do we read Catholic literature?), and the result can easily be that we close our minds and our hearts to the suffering in the world around us.

Respecting Differences

We will never again have a church in which everyone thinks and acts alike. We are now more attuned to the different ways God's Spirit moves in people. Different personalities will respond differently.

Some will put their trust in order and organization; others will not be gifted in those areas but may be moved to present ideas and dreams. Some will be great thinkers; others will not be strong on logic and creative ideas but will have hearts of profound compassion. Some will give priority to law and authority, while others will challenge that law and authority in the name of the Gospel. We need to expect and respect these differences. Too often the differences become distorted by hardened hearts, closed minds, and an abiding dislike for people who think and act differently.

There cannot be an "only way" for the Spirit of God to act in people. By all means let us defend strongly the way each of us perceives the Spirit to be acting in the church. Others may not agree with us and may argue strongly against us. We should be prepared to accept that. Sometimes the issue will be different ways of seeing things and making judgments — and with it, differing attitudes toward what has most importance. So, for one person, respect for church law might be high on a scale of importance, while for another person that value may not be as important as compassion for people who are hurting.

It is inevitable, then, that they differ on some issues, e.g., divorce and remarriage.

The same differences are evident when Catholics discuss aspects of Catholic teaching that are not essential to the following of Jesus. Two women, for example, discuss purgatory. One says she believes in it because it is clear church teaching; she expects to spend some time in a "place" after death being purified before she can come into the presence of God; she feels disturbed when she hears other Catholics calling into question what has always been a strong part of her Catholic faith. The other woman says,

> When my husband was dying he asked me to forgive him any wrong he had done to me in our thirty-one years of marriage. I held him, and deep within my heart yearned for him to know how utterly I forgave him. My embrace and words told him of my love and forgiveness. I thought later that if I could love him so deeply and forgive him so completely — and un-questioningly — how much more readily and totally must God have done so when they met. Isn't that the idea of God Jesus tells us to have?

The second woman is plainly questioning the traditional notion of purgatory. She is confident her husband is immediately embraced by a loving God.

There are differences like these among us that should not be used as a test whether someone is a "loyal" Catholic or not. It is a sad feature of present-day Catholicism to find men and woman under attack because they bring the fruits of their scholarship and new insights to our faith. Some groups or organizations seem to have set themselves up as watchdogs of what makes a person a "loyal" Catholic. The refusal to tolerate another point of view is often quite strong in such groups. This intolerance, when brought to bear on issues that allow for differences of opinion, should have no place in the church community.

There is, here, a challenge for people who like to work with the hierarchical model of the church in which authority works from the top down: the listen and obey model. The challenge is to allow differences — and to *encourage* those who are different. In listening to and learning from gifted people who are different, we can all cooperate better with the Spirit and face the reality of change rather than trying to prevent it.

On the other hand, there is an equal challenge to those who want change and who thrive on it. Change is empty unless it is well grounded. The grounding for change in the church is Scripture and the church's tradition and teaching. People advocating change should be familiar with these sources. They should be able to show how change is faithful to those sources of our faith.

Conclusion

In these and the other challenges facing the church we return to the central point of Jesus' teaching: *God is with you*. He addressed this message again and again to people *outside* the Law, the sinners and the social outcasts. While stating that he had not come to abolish the Law, he clearly saw that a legalistic mentality kept blocking the influence of God's love. Jesus went beyond this and touched the lives of people who thought God could not be close to them. He affirmed the closeness, and he instructed them to stop sinning. In other words, they were to live in the belief that God was close and witness to that in what they did, especially in keeping the great commandment of Love. As church we are called to follow St. Paul's instruction: "In your minds you must be the same as Jesus Christ" (Phil. 2:5). The church must present the mind — and the heart — of Jesus to its followers and to the world. We are to break with attitudes and practices with which Jesus would not associate.

Individually, each of us is called to put our faith in that message of Jesus. He calls us to live life with all its ups and downs confident of God's closeness, and to allow that belief and that love to move us beyond the limits we so often put on our love and our concern for others.

The church nurtures, supports, sustains, and encourages us. But it is you and I who, in a real sense, must carry the church. We are to make its presence strong in our world through our belief in and response to God's loving presence with us. In doing this we will then witness in our living what St. John proclaimed:

> We ourselves have known
> and put our faith in God's love for us.
> God is love,
> and whoever lives in love lives in God,
> and God lives in them.
>
> (1 John 4:16)

Summary

- The nature of authority is a key issue in the way the church is perceived.

- "Unbelief" and "poor presentation" were traced to the pyramid style of church, authority being remote from people, and the role of the people being to listen and obey.

- In early church experience, the "Communio" style involved people as bearers of the Spirit. Authority was closer to the people.

- Renewal in the church is grounded in a reexamination of early tradition and the truth that all are gifted with God's presence. Laity were not passive spectators in the early church.

- Leadership must lead people to see themselves as gifted and empowered by God's Spirit.

Chapter 5

Prayer: Deepening Our Awareness of God's Nearness

Before reading this chapter, you might like to spend a few moments reflecting on the following questions:

1. Do you *want* to learn to pray better?

2. How much time are you prepared to give to this?

I HAVE SEVERAL STRONG CONVICTIONS about prayer:

- We should be praying.

- There is no *one way* to pray.

- It is not essential to have a lot of time.

- We will not find a formula or technique that will make prayer always easy.

- There are, however, various ways of praying that can make the activity more fruitful.

The activity we call prayer embraces a wide range of styles and types. This final chapter will concentrate on some prayer styles that may be helpful in deepening

- our awareness of God's love and presence,

- our relationship with the human and divine Jesus, and

- our awareness of ourselves as bearers of the sacred.

Deepening Awareness of God's Love and Presence

This prayer style focuses on *listening and being attentive to* the words God's Spirit speaks to us through Scripture.

> Listen, listen to me. . . .
> Pay attention, come to me,
> listen, and your soul will live. (Isa. 55:3)

> I tell you most solemnly,
> whoever listens to my words
> and believes in the one who sent me,
> has eternal life. (John 5:24)

The importance of listening to Scripture is clear. Where and how to start is often the difficulty. However, with attention to some simple points, praying with the help of Scripture is something anyone can easily do.

Begin your prayer by asking God for a deeper awareness of God's love for you and God's presence with you.

Have in mind that your prayer will be simple rather than difficult or complex. Give yourself space, time, and quietness, and take some time to relax yourself with some gentle breathing. A simple exercise like imagining you are breathing in God's Spirit can be helpful. Then settle down with a passage you have chosen from Scripture. Choose the passage beforehand. Read it through and get the feel of it. Then take it slowly phrase by phrase and personalize it: imagine God speaking the words to you. Let God use your name often. Do not be concerned by distraction. Rather, when distracted, be gentle with yourself and return to the text.

Do not search out meanings in the text or new insights. Seek a *heart* rather than a head experience. Let your God speak to your heart. Be content to pause, to move very slowly. You do not need to "get something out of" the time in prayer. Let it simply be a restful time with the God who loves you and is with you. Above all, let God speak to you rather than speaking to God yourself.

Be attentive to what is in your heart as you read and listen, and respond gently with words of thanks or joy or contentment. Do not race on to what you should be doing if you really believe that God loves you. Stay with the reality of that love. Enjoy it! Surely God would want that!

This sort of prayer has been likened to floating in water. To float requires relaxation and trust. Too often in prayer we tense up or use words like a drowning person pounding the water. We think *we* have to make the prayer work. Rather, we should simply be there, open to God's presence, allowing God to speak to our hearts, and letting our response be gentle and grateful.

This is not *the* way to pray. It is *one* way. It is a good way to pray when life is on a fairly even keel. It is a good way to deepen our awareness of God's love. It should have a place in our prayer life.

Personalizing the texts is important. Some of the texts will be speaking about God. Change these texts to God speaking to you. For example, Ephesians 2:4–7 speaks of God's great love for us: "But God loved us so much that he was generous with his mercy: when we were dead through our sins, he brought us to life." Imagine God wanting to tell you that. Let God speak your name. Imagine God saying, "John/Mary, I love you with so much love." Or change the words slightly while keeping the intention of the passage, for example, "John/Mary, I love you with a love that will never end."

The beauty of using Scripture in prayer is that it gives the mind and heart something to focus on. And it is the fruit of God's Spirit at work in our world.

The appendix (p. 119) contains references to the Old and New Testaments that can be used for this type of prayer.

Relating with Jesus in Prayer

One way to get to know Jesus, the man, better would be to take time occasionally to reflect on a Gospel incident, trying to be in touch with what Jesus might be feeling. It is like trying to get inside his skin and sensing what he might have felt. This is not far-fetched. It is a simple way of getting in touch with his humanness. In some incidents this is easy, as when he cries over Jerusalem or in chapter 4 of Mark's Gospel where we read, "Grieved to find them so obstinate, he looked angrily around at them." We could imagine the scene and simply ask the question, "Were you really angry, Jesus?" and try to stay with his mood or feeling.

Another form of prayer is to imagine yourself in a scene, meeting Jesus. For example, if you take the incident of Jesus meeting the blind man, imagine yourself there instead of the blind person. The important part of the prayer is allowing yourself to "meet" Jesus, allowing him to be with you, to look at you, touch you, speak to you.

Often the Gospel does not tell us how Jesus feels. But our own human experience can give us a good idea of how he might have felt. Let us look at two brief passages in the Gospels and see how our own experience can be a stepping stone into the heart of Jesus.

The first passage is from Mark's Gospel (3:20–21):

> He went home again, and once more such a crowd collected that they could not even have a meal. When his relatives heard of this, they set out to take charge of him, convinced he was out of his mind.

His relatives thought he was mad, out of his mind. They wanted to lock him up. Here is a sentence in the Gospel where we could stop sometime and imagine what it must have been like for Jesus. He had good news he wanted to share, and his own relations rejected him. The questions from our own experience could be:

- Do I know what it is like to be misunderstood or rejected?

- Do I know what it is to have relatives reject the values I hold dear?

- Do I know what it is like to want to share something precious to me with people close to me and they are not interested?

We might not have got to the stage where our relatives want to lock us up, but we can imagine what it must have felt like for Jesus. Could we, then, sit with him for a few moments in prayer and be with what it must have been like for him? We can make the mistake of thinking that he would not have been deeply touched by it all.

The second passage is in Matthew (14:12–13):

> John's disciples came and took John's body and buried it; then they went off to tell Jesus. When Jesus received the news he withdrew by boat to a lonely place where they could be by themselves.

Clearly, Jesus is deeply disturbed. Imagine you are with Jesus when the men arrive and tell him that John has been murdered. What do you sense happening in Jesus as they relate how John died? Imagine you are left alone with Jesus afterward, before the boat ride. What is he feeling? It could be any number of deep feelings: shock, anger, regret, fear, powerlessness, loneliness, helplessness, abandonment, rage, concern, grief.

If you follow on with this incident in the Gospel, what is it like to be with Jesus on the boat trip across the lake? What must it be like for Jesus when he gets mobbed on the other side when he's clearly desperate for solitude and reflection? What do you imagine Jesus prays about that night when he goes to the mountain alone? *Be there, and be with him.* Be *close,* like a friend.

This form of reflection and prayer is a very good way to respond to Jesus' invitation, "Come and learn of my heart."

Another prayer form develops from our willingness to reflect prayerfully on Jesus' humanness. This type of prayer is one we can use often. It need not be lengthy, and it will develop awareness of our closeness with Jesus. It is simply this: whenever you go to prayer and are aware of some strong feeling within you, begin with the feeling and let it be the stepping stone to Jesus. For example, when you feel frustrated or dead tired, disappointed or lonely, whatever the feeling, let it surface as the reality of your life now, and ask Jesus if he ever felt what you are now feeling. The purpose of the prayer is not to ask Jesus to remove the painful reality of your life, but to share it with him as friend and companion. This sharing with him is an excellent means of developing real friendship with him. Surely he wants that!

Again, it is important in this type of prayer to resolve to *be with him* and not to rush on to what you ought to be doing. There are times when praying this type of prayer that the Spirit will surprise us with some insight or jog our conscience. Leave it to the Spirit! The type of prayer that thinks about a Gospel passage and then looks for a resolution or an application to life is *not* the prayer being described here. That prayer style has great value, but it should be clearly distinguished from this prayer of *being with* Jesus.

Some passages for use in this type of prayer will be found in the appendix (see p. 122).

Prayer: Awareness of the Spirit of God in Our Lives

Prayer often needs to be accompanied with some discipline to safeguard its regularity and length. Sometimes, though, particularly with regard to the length of the prayer time, discipline may have the effect of killing prayer. This can happen when someone determines to pray, for example, for forty-five minutes, and no matter how dry the prayer, the forty-five minutes is adhered to. Sometimes that is a good thing and serves a worthwhile goal. On the other hand, there is something to be said for a simple prayer that tries to capture in a few minutes an awareness of God's presence.

This simple prayer has its foundation in scriptural statements such as "We are the earthenware jars that hold a treasure," "We are temples of God's Holy Spirit." In other words, we are "tabernacles," each one of us. The same sacred reality we genuflect to in the church is within us, a part of who we are. This is a truth, a reality of our lives, that we need to touch again and again. If we can do it simply, why not try to do so?

Take a few minutes to get comfortable and to relax. Imagine the Spirit of God speaking to you, using your name, and saying something like, "Mary/John, I live in you," or "I make my home in you." Even if it is only for a few moments, try to be with the reality that this is true for you; it is a part of your very being.

Relish it and be thankful. Avoid the mistake of rushing into an examination of conscience. For the moment stay with the affirmation and the encouragement of God's Spirit with you.

The call to witness will eventually grow out of this deepened awareness of the Spirit of God's closeness. A feature of this will be the conviction, acquired in this prayer, that the Spirit of God never leaves us, never gives up on us, even when we fail.

Prayer: Awareness That We Share in God's Love

The following statements form the foundation of another simple prayer style. The power of the prayer rests on the belief we give to these statements, most of which are found in Scripture, especially in the writings of John.

- God is love.

- We are created in the image of God.

- We are the only creatures who can love; we are blessed with intelligence, will, memory, and imagination to help us love.

- To be created in the image of Love Itself means that our loving is a sharing in God's own life.

- Our loving, then, can give us our best understanding of what God is like.

- Reflecting on our loving can give us a deeply prayerful experience of God's closeness.

- "As long as we love one another, God will live in us." (1 John 4:12)

- "God is love, and whoever loves lives in God and God lives in them." (1 John 4:16)

- Our God is as intimate with us, as much a part of us, as our loving.

- "You are to love one another the way I have loved you." (John 15:12)

We are to love one another just as Jesus loved. Put in another way we can understand this truth to mean that when we love we are bringing God's loving presence to one another. Let us be attentive, then, to those we most love and be aware in this attentiveness how God is loving in and through us. We could ask: To whom do I bring God's loving presence in my loving?

Christians are called to see the close connection between their everyday loving and the presence of God with them. Yet, so often, good, deeply loving and faithful people think themselves to be at a distance from God!

The basis of this simple prayer is to sit quietly and bring to mind one or several people whom we love, and be with the awareness that in loving them we are bringing God's love to them.

On the one hand, this prayer should be encouraging, uplifting, tinged with wonder. It should not set out to be an examination of conscience that slips quickly into focusing on how we are failing. No, stay with the positive aspect and take delight in the mystery and the wonder of it:

- God is with me.

- God is loving others through me.

On the other hand, we do fail in our loving. We all know we can and should love better. What will happen as we sit with the positive aspect of our loving, developing our awareness of the truth of God's presence with us, is that the Spirit of God will gently, and at times surprisingly, reveal a challenge to love someone better. It is important, though, to leave that in the hands of the Spirit. The Spirit of God can and will break through into our awareness if we enter the prayer positively.

There are times when we do need to sit and ask ourselves where we are failing in our loving. However, it is a very common tendency for people to slip quickly into reflection on their failure, making resolutions for the future, and losing the positive aspect. Prayer should in some way reflect the way Jesus taught: be *positive* first. *Believe* the Good News, and then give witness to it. We must give ourselves space and time to hear and believe the Good News about God's love for us and presence with us. We can test our experience of prayer: How much time have we put into feeling guilty and being conscious of failure and our distance from God as against the time we have put into deepening our awareness, prayerfully, that God loves us, is with us, and loves through us? The responsibility for that is in our hands. If we choose to pray and have the will to give some time to it, even a small amount of time, then we can change the pattern of our prayer.

Prayer: Unredeemed Prayers

We are redeemed people — set free from religious thought patterns and images that enslave and bind people into fear, despair, and notions that God is not close to us. Our prayers should reflect this reality. Why, then, do so many of the prayers that we pray, liturgically, devotionally, privately, and in sharing with one another, indicate that we have not been set free? Why do so many of them indicate a belief that our God is not close to us? Why do we allow so many prayers to keep coming from a bad theology of unworthiness?

We would do well to look carefully at the prayers we say, privately and collectively (especially at liturgy) and see the thought patterns that shape them. Almost every Sunday we pray prayers that reinforce the belief that God is not close to us or that we have to *ask* God to be loving, kind, merciful. Here are some examples from a seven-week stretch in Sundays of Ordinary Time:

- In Week 4 we pray, "Bless this people with the gift of your kingdom." Has God not done this yet?

- The next Sunday we ask God to "watch over your family." Isn't God doing that?

- In Week 6 we ask God to "help us to live in your presence." Maybe God would want to reply that the help has been given but we won't believe in it!

- The following Sunday again finds us asking God to "Help us...."

- In Week 8 we ask God to "form in us the likeness of your Son."

- Week 9 calls on God to "hear our call."

- Week 10 finds us asking God to "send your Spirit to teach us your truth."

- And in Week 11 we again ask God to "help us...."

The prayer after communion in Week 14 actually asks God to "give us a share in your life."

What attitudes are we reinforcing week after week when we begin or end our Eucharist with such prayers? Would it not be far more uplifting, encouraging, and true to our understanding of salvation to make the prayers positive, for example:

- You *have blessed us* with the gift of your kingdom. May we....

- You *watch* over us....

- You are *always present* to help us....

- You *have shared* your Spirit with us....

- You *have given* us a share in your life....

We could be led then from this awareness to be challenged to give witness to it in our lives. We might then avoid another type of prayer that asks God to do what we ought to be doing *with God's help,* for example, working for peace or justice in the world around us. There is much prayer that is simply cozy escapism, such as asking God to care for the sick, the elderly, the unemployed, the broken-hearted. Week after week parishioners hear Prayers of the Faithful in this vein. The challenge is surely to us, as bearers of God's love, to be present to the needy. Prayers that do not affirm God's presence with us and do not challenge us to witness to that presence run the risk of being unchristian on the one hand and pure escapism on the other.

There is clearly a place for what is called Prayer of Petition — the prayer that asks God for grace and favor. In many cases, though, a little attention to our attitudes and the way we frame our prayers could make a great difference. Take, for example, the case of Aunt Nellie who is very sick. A usual type of prayer asks God to "be with" her or "grant her a quick recovery." While that type of prayer can be most rewarding for Aunt Nellie and those who pray it, it runs the risk of (a) indicating that God is not active unless we ask, and (b) leaving it all to God.

An alternative form of prayer could be along the lines, "God of life. You are always lovingly present to us and Aunt Nellie. We pray that in her sickness she may have a deep awareness of your presence with her and be strengthened by it. We commit ourselves to helping her with our love and kindness."

Conclusion

God is near to us, whether we believe this or not. This is part of the truth of our lives. It is the truth God speaks to us in Scripture. It is the Good News preached by Jesus. We may disagree on ways to express this, ways to celebrate it, and ways the community we call church lives it, but we must not deny the truth of it. We must hear it; we must believe it. If we do not hear and believe it, we will not witness to it.

And if we do not witness to it, our church fails.

> "I chose you;
> and I commissioned you
> to go out and bear fruit."
> (John 15:16)

Appendix

Scripture Texts for Prayer Developing Awareness of God's Love for Us

OLD TESTAMENT

Genesis 28:15–17

"Know that I am with you and will keep you wherever you go, and will bring you back to this land; for I will not leave you until I have done what I have promised you."

Then Jacob woke from his sleep and said, "Surely the LORD is in this place — and I did not know it!" And he was afraid, and said, "How awesome is this place! This is none other than the house of God, and this is the gate of heaven."

Numbers 6:22–27

The Lord spoke to Moses, saying: Speak to Aaron and his sons, saying, "Thus you shall bless the Israelites: You shall say to them,

The Lord bless you and keep you;
the Lord make his face to shine upon you, and be
gracious to you;

119

the Lord lift up his countenance upon you, and give
you peace.
So they shall put my name on the Israelites, and I
will bless them."

Lamentations 3:22–26

The steadfast love of the LORD never ceases, his mercies
never come to an end; they are new every morning; great
is your faithfulness. "The LORD is my portion," says my
soul, "therefore I will hope in him." The LORD is good to
those who wait for him, to the soul that seeks him. It is
good that one should wait quietly for the salvation of the
LORD.

Zephaniah 3:14–18

Sing aloud, O daughter Zion; shout, O Israel! Rejoice and
exult with all your heart, O daughter Jerusalem! The LORD
has taken away the judgments against you, he has turned
away your enemies. The king of Israel, the LORD, is in
your midst; you shall fear disaster no more. On that day it
shall be said to Jerusalem: Do not fear, O Zion; do not let
your hands grow weak. The LORD, your God, is in your
midst, a warrior who gives victory; he will rejoice over you
with gladness, he will renew you in his love; he will exult
over you with loud singing as on a day of festival.

Other Suggested Old Testament Texts

Deuteronomy 1:29–32; 7:6–9; 30:4, 11, 14, 15–20;
32:10–11

Judges 6:11–18

1 Samuel 16:6–7

2 Samuel 7:5–12, 18–29

1 Kings 8:56–61

Psalms 1:3; 3:3–5; Ps. 8; Ps. 16; 18:1, 18, 28–29; Ps. 27; 28:7; 40:1–7, 11, 16–17; 46:10; Ps. 62; 65:9–13; 73:23–28; 89:1–4, 26–28; Ps. 91; 94:18–22; Ps. 100; Ps. 103; Ps. 121; Ps. 131; 132:13–14; Ps. 139; Ps. 145; 146:1–2

Song of Songs 2:10–16

Wisdom 6:12–17; 7:22–30; 9:10–11; 11:24–26

Ecclesiasticus 24:3–30

Isaiah chap. 12; 25:1, 6–10; 30:18–26; 32:15; 35:3–10; 38:16–17; 40:9–11, 28–31; 41:9–14, 17–20; 43:1–5; 44:1–3, 21–23; 45:2–6, 15; 46:3–4; 49:1–5, 8–16; 54:5, 8, 10; All of chap. 55; 57:15, 18–19; 60:19–20; 62:3–5, 11–12; 63:7–9, 14; 65:17–19

Jeremiah 1:4–8; 18:1–6; 29:11–14; 31:2–4, 31–34; 32:39–41; 33:3, 6–7, 9–11

Baruch 5:1–3, 9

Ezekiel 11:19–21; 34:11–16; 36:24–36; 37:1–14; 47:1–12

Daniel 3:40–43 (not in Good News Bible and some others)

Hosea 2:14–24; 6:1–4; 11:1–4, 8–9; 14:5–9

Joel 2:23–27; 3:1

NEW TESTAMENT

1 Corinthians 3:16–17

Do you not know that you are God's temple and that God's Spirit dwells in you? If anyone destroys God's temple, God will destroy that person. For God's temple is holy, and you are that temple.

Ephesians 3:16–21

I pray that, according to the riches of his glory, he may grant that you may be strengthened in your inner being with power through his Spirit, and that Christ may dwell in your hearts through faith, as you are being rooted and grounded in love. I pray that you may have the power to comprehend, with all the saints, what is the breadth and length and height and depth, and to know the love of Christ that surpasses knowledge, so that you may be filled with all the fullness of God. Now to him who by the power at work within us is able to accomplish abundantly far more than all we can ask or imagine, to him be glory in the church and in Christ Jesus to all generations, forever and ever. Amen.

Colossians 1:27–29

To them God chose to make known how great among the Gentiles are the riches of the glory of this mystery, which is Christ in you, the hope of glory. It is he whom we proclaim, warning everyone and teaching everyone in all wisdom, so that we may present everyone mature in Christ. For this I toil and struggle with all the energy that he powerfully inspires within me.

Other Suggested New Testament Texts

John's Gospel chapters 15–17

Romans 5:1–11; chap. 8; 10:8–10

1 Corinthians 1:4–9, 26–31; 12:1–22; chap. 13

2 Corinthians 1:3–7; 4:7–11; 5:18–6:2; 12:7–10; 13:3–6

Galatians 1:15; 2:18–21; 4:3–9; 5:16–26

Ephesians chap. 1; 2:4–10; 4:1–12

Philippians 1:2–11; 2:1–11; 3:7–11; 4:4–9, 12–13

Colossians 1:9–14; 3:3–4, 9–15

1 Timothy 1:12–17

2 Timothy 1:6–7

Titus 3:4–7

1 Peter 1:3–9; 2:9–10

2 Peter 1:3–11

1 John chap. 1; 3:1; 4:7–21

Revelation 3:7–13; 21:1–8; 22:1–2, 17–21

Notes

1. John Paul II, *Reconciliatio et Paenitentia of John Paul II to the Bishops, Clergy and Faithful on Reconciliation and Penance in the Mission of the Church Today* (Homebush, NSW, Australia: St. Paul Publications, 1985), 66. Available online at www.intratext.com/X/ENG0117.htm.

2. See the Office of Readings, Saturday, Week 9 of the year. The second reading is from the commentary of St. Thomas Aquinas on John's Gospel. The quote from St. Augustine is also found here.

3. St. Teresa of Jesus, *The Life of Teresa of Jesus,* trans. E. Allison Peers (New York: Doubleday, 1960), 214.

4. Joseph M. Powers, S.J., *Eucharistic Theology* (New York: Herder and Herder, 1967), 26.

5. Constitution on the Sacred Liturgy no. 11, *Documents of Vatican II,* ed. Walter Abbott, S.J. (London: Geoffrey Chapman, 1967).

6. See Yves Congar, "Letter from Father Yves Congar, O.P.," in *Theology Digest* (Fall 1985): 213.

7. Ibid., 214.

8. Karl Rahner, *The Shape of the Church to Come* (New York: Seabury Press, 1974), 82.

9. Ibid.

10. Ibid., 24.

11. Avery Dulles, *A Church to Believe In* (New York: Crossroad, 1985), 3.

12. Ibid.

13. See Dolores Leckey, "What the Laity Need," in *Origins* (May 20, 1982): 14.

14. Rosemary Haughton, quoted in *Catholic Beliefs and Practices,* ed. Carmel Leavey, O.P., and Margaret Hetherton (Melbourne: Collins Dove, 1988), 113.

15. Henri Nouwen, *The Wounded Healer* (New York: Doubleday, 1972), 39.

16. Nathan Mitchell, "The Sense of the Sacred," in *Parish: A Place for Worship,* ed. Mark Searle (Collegeville, Minn.: Liturgical Press, 1980), 78.

17. "Report on Parish Liturgical Celebrations," *Origins* (October 31, 1985): 334.

Of related interest by
HENRI J. M. NOUWEN

THE HEART OF HENRI NOUWEN

In commemoration of the 70th anniversary of Nouwen's birth, Crossroad issues this anthology of the best of Henri Nouwen from our list: *Life of the Beloved; Here and Now; Beyond the Mirror; Finding My Way Home;* and *Sabbatical Journey.* This collection focuses on the three themes that were closest to his own heart: hope in suffering, a personal relationship with God, and living for others.

0-8245-1985-X, $18.95 hardcover

BEYOND THE MIRROR
Reflections on Death and Life

Beyond the Mirror, about Nouwen's near death experience in 1989, has been unavailable since 1997. This new edition includes a Foreword by Robert Durback and an Afterword from the Henri Nouwen Archives about preparing for death.

0-8245-1961-2; $14.95 paperback

LIFE OF THE BELOVED
Spiritual Living in a Secular World

"One day while walking on Columbus Avenue in New York City, Fred turned to me and said, 'Why don't you write something about the spiritual life for me and my friends?'

"Fred's question became more than the intriguing suggestion of a young New York intellectual. It became the plea that arose on all sides — wherever I was open to hear it. And, in the end, it became for me the most pertinent and the most urgent of all demands: 'Speak to us about God.'"   *–From the Prologue*

0-8245-1184-0, $15.95 hardcover

crossroad

crossroad

Field Fences
405 W Main